I'm not sure I've ever read a book on Leadership that so accurately diagnoses what transpires in a Leader/Follower relationship. Leading at Mach 2 was a thrill from start to finish!
—Jerry Jasinowski
   President, National Association of Manufacturers

Leading at Mach 2 is just another example of Steve Sullivan's uncanny ability to get to the heart of the issue. This "work of art," by one of America's best, gives the reader a fascinating perspective on a subject that is critical to organizational success.
—Christian Holmes
   Executive Director, Environment, Health, Safety, Tenneco

What could have been more appropriate and timely as a sequel to *Selling at Mach 1* than *Leading at Mach 2*. Steve Sullivan is one of the most dynamic leaders in industry today and his willingness to share his recipe for success makes reading his new book a "must."
—David S. Dimling
   Group Vice President, Georgia-Pacific Corporation

A tour de force!
—Phil F. McLaughlin
   CEO, McLaughlin & Associates

I saw the title *Leading at Mach 2* and thought, "what could an author know about leadership." Now that I have completed it, I realize . . . everything!
—Thomas A. Steiner
   Chairman of the Board, Advance Business Graphics

Steve Sullivan may lead at Mach 2, but he delivers his message at Mach 4.
—Laurence B. Mindel
   Chairman and Chief Executive Officer, Il Fornaio Corporation

The leader's number one job is to create a clear vision that excites and motivates. Steve Sullivan's compelling new book not only shows you how but tells you why.
—C. D. Peterson
   Author, *Staying in Demand*

LEADING

AT

MACH 2

STEVE SULLIVAN

Edinburgh Press
New York San Francisco Stockholm

A Motivational Resources Book
54 Danbury Road, Suite 308
Ridgefield, Connecticut 06877
in association with Edinburgh Press
Stockholm, Sweden

Advisor and Creative Consultant, Amy J. Pecora

Book Cover Design by Patti Britton
Britton Designs, Sonoma, California
Chapter Illustrations by Maria Lauricella
New York, New York

10 9 8 7 6 5 4 3

ISBN: 0-9641053-2-2 (hardcover)
      0-9641053-1-4 (paperback)

**To purchase additional copies,
please write or call:
Motivational Resources
54 Danbury Road, Suite 308
Ridgefield, Connecticut 06877
203-438-5952**

CONTENTS

To Leaders
And
Those That Follow

To My Dad
Who Taught Me The Importance Of Both

FOREWORD

I spend my working hours helping private industry and government clients transform their enterprises into balanced, high-performance organizations. They are keenly focused on mastering change to stay on top and excel at what they do. Because it is no easy task, everyone is looking for "silver bullet," quick-fix solutions that can provide miracle breakthroughs. Having spent my career focusing on issues of business reengineering, total quality management, downsizing and outsourcing, I have long held the belief that simple solutions to complex problems just don't exist. That was until I read Steve Sullivan's *Leading at Mach 2*.

Steve Sullivan, ex-Army Ranger, entrepreneur, senior corporate executive, sportsman, adventurer, father and friend, has supplied all of us with a map and compass for leading and building superior organizations. It doesn't matter whether you're the CEO of a mega-conglomerate, a four-star general, a parent, a priest or chairman of the local PTA, *Leading at Mach 2* provides a pathfinder's wisdom on what it takes to create a Mach 2 environment of outstanding leadership.

Thousands of books have been written on the subject of leadership, going all the way back to the Bible when Adam made the original bad leadership decision. Caesar, as Steve reminds us, lost an empire due to poor leadership. After winning a key battle, Napoleon is reputed to have said, "I have learned something marvelous today. Men will give me their lives for a simple piece of ribbon and metal."

Leading at Mach 2 proves that Napoleon was wrong. I am convinced that if he had read this keystone work on leadership, Napoleon's battle at Waterloo may have had a different outcome than defeat. *Leading at Mach 2* has no complex techniques, gimmicks or academic theories that seem to be so popular in the many of today's books on the subject. That's because Steve's brand of leadership is based on seemingly simple and familiar words, yet very difficult-to-master eternal truths: integrity, loyalty, trust, respect, responsibility, support, care and commitment.

"Leadership," Steve tells us, "is about looking out for someone else." At first glance, this is a strange, tender message coming from a very tough guy who has literally jumped out of airplanes, rappelled down icy cliffs, marched and slept in sub-zero weather, and survived and thrived in snake-infested jungles, while many of us preferred to stay home. Steve has been there and done it.

Today, many other people have been there and done it because of Steve Sullivan. The common thread that runs through much of what he has accomplished is that people have willingly followed him. And, in return, he has led them to a higher level of personal performance.

Whether it was a young, inexperienced Army private shooting a grenade launcher, a nervous salesman giving his first presentation, or a girls' softball team making its debut, Steve has been at their side, leading by creating energy in each of them. If you have been lucky enough to have met some of his followers, as I have, you know the phenomena I am describing. By merely mentioning his name to such people, a smile crosses their face. It is the smile of quiet self-confidence, a smile grown from an experience with Steve, a smile created and endowed with the energy of true leadership.

When you've finished his thesis I suspect you will know how to create this energy yourself. By applying his recipe for leadership success it won't be long before you also are LEADING AT MACH 2.

— Burnes P. Hollyman

A PERSONAL OBSERVATION

The day I received the call from Edinburgh Press, I was surprised. While I've known Steve Sullivan for over twenty years, my contact with him this past decade has been limited. The caller stated he had received instructions to get in touch with me, to see if I would be a contributor to *Leading at Mach 2*. When I asked why, he said it had to do with Steve's respect for my leadership ability.

I was doubly flattered, because not only did it appear that I had made an impression on Steve, but my involvement with him had been so long ago, it was hard to believe he still remembered.

I told him I'd be happy to participate. After receiving my copy of the manuscript, I ingested it word by word. Upon finishing, I was disappointed because I had nothing left to add. I then realized you will hear enough about leadership from the author, so maybe it would be appropriate to hear something about him from me.

I remember the day he arrived at the 197th Infantry Brigade, at Ft. Benning, Georgia, in 1974. My personnel officer informed me a "hot shot" young captain had just signed in and asked if I would welcome him. We exchanged pleasantries, and I went back to work.

My first real conversation with Steve occurred at one of my staff meetings. The Ft. Benning flag football season was about to begin, and he was the quarterback and coach of our Headquarter's team. At the end of the meeting, I asked him how we would do. He said, matter of factly, that we would win the championship. Given the four hundred teams in the league, I thought the statement was a bit bold.

Three months later, when Steve accepted the championship trophy on behalf of the Brigade, I had a feeling it was the start of my association with a lifetime of Sullivan successes. The year and a half he was under my command, I saw him transform everything he touched. Now, whether I'm reading about him in the *New York Times*, listening to his opinions on talk radio, buying Osoli apparel or engulfed in one of his books, I continue to marvel at the speed at which he is able to accomplish things.

To be honest, there were times when I was a little envious of his success. For years my wife, Ute, has suspected something was up. She said more than once, no one could do all that he has done by himself. After reading *Leading at Mach 2*, it's obvious she was right. He didn't!

— Godwin Ordway

PROLOGUE

I don't know how many books you've read on the subject of leadership, but I suspect quite a few. I know I have, and yet I'm still searching for that one dissertation that holds the secrets to the universe. I had no idea how difficult the journey would be.

My trip on the path to enlightenment got so tiresome a few years back, I pulled into a rest stop. As I contemplated the issue, I realized I would never find, The Book. The best I could hope for would be a pearl of wisdom here, an intellectual jewel there and a whole lot of experiential learning in between.

It's not that the answers don't exist, they're readily available. Read the ten best books on the subject and you will find a solution to every leadership challenge. Digging them out is the easy part. Resolution is another issue. It has something to do with the nature of problems. They're always more difficult to resolve after they've had time to take root.

It's for that reason, in *Leading at Mach 2*, that I take a proactive approach. I'm not as concerned with cures as I am with prevention. It's my belief with the proper inoculation you will never suffer a leadership malady.

At no time do I draw conclusions, speculate on possible outcomes or assume anything. To use a miller's vernacular, the chaff has been discarded in favor of the wheat, but only after it proved to be worthless. What remains is my view of what it takes to lead others and accomplish your objectives in a minimal amount of time.

Leading at Mach 2

INTRODUCTION

Books are written for many reasons, and as I sit here I'm wondering why I'm going through the process again. My motivation has nothing to do with the fact that *Selling at Mach 1*, has been a success. I had never planned on being a writer. Only smart people wrote books.

My first literary effort occurred by accident. One morning my phone rang and the caller inquired if I would come to Brussels to address a group of Defense Department managers on the subject of business.

I asked how long he wanted me to speak and he replied, three hours. I had kept audiences awake for an hour but this involved triple time without a corresponding pay incentive. I said okay. To make a short story shorter, by the time I organized my thoughts, I had a lot of material. Enough that it resembled a manuscript.

On the flight over, a gentleman across the aisle asked about the subject of my book. I started to explain it wasn't a book, but then a light went on. Why not? Writers get great seats in restaurants. "It's about taking care of customers," I replied. There, I've done it, I committed myself. Write another hundred pages, add a cover, and Ruth Sullivan could call her son an author.

At no time during its creation did my palms get sweaty, my brow perspire or my breathing become labored. As happy as I am with the finished product, I admit, I wrote it without passion. I merely played the role of a conduit through which information flowed. I presented the modus operandi of successful salespeople from a conceptual standpoint. Take it or leave it. If readers chose not to embrace my message, it was their prerogative.

Leading at Mach 2 is a different issue: This book will be written with all the passion I can muster. I'm passionate about excellence. I'm passionate about how organizations serve their employees. I'm passionate about how they support their efforts. I'm passionate about recognizing performance. I'm passionate about rewarding accomplishment. And, finally, I'm overwhelmingly passionate about holding individuals accountable for their actions.

My passion did not arrive conveniently before some speech. It has grown within me for the past twenty-three years. In that period of time I have had fourteen different jobs. I mention it only because virtually every assignment I've been given has involved resolving conflict. I've replaced individuals who may not have been criminal but certainly were inept, and by cleaning up their mistakes, I have learned a lot about leadership.

In the course of this presentation I will juxtapose the best with the worst and let you be the critic. My mission is simple. It has one objective: to make you a better leader. No, that's not correct. Better is a relative state of affairs. I want to make you an outstanding leader. Your actions and ultimately the performance of your people will measure up against any qualitative yardstick.

Leading at Mach 2 is not for everyone, but it is for anyone who is committed to making their organization better, by optimizing the performance of their most important asset . . . the human resource.

BOOK STATEMENT

Leadership does not materialize as a result of good intention. Its genesis comes with an understanding that action is the catalyst for change. Leadership starts with an attitude that nothing holds greater worth than the commitment you make to those you lead. It ends with the belief you have done your best on their behalf. As your knowledge about leadership grows, you will come to realize, accomplishment is more than just success, it is also a validation of energy created along the way.

EGG OR
CLASSROOM

He was so learned that he could name
a horse in nine languages; so ignorant
he bought a cow to ride on.
— Benjamin Franklin

W hy is it so many people don't lead? It's not as if what needs to be done hasn't been addressed for ages. Just ask Machiavelli; he'll be happy to share his thoughts with you. Information on the subject is everywhere. Sign up for a leadership training seminar, and if you don't get there early, you won't get a seat.

The participants are concerned, energetic and committed. They take notes, ask questions and get answers. They leave their educational experience with hope and anticipation and can't wait to implement what they've learned. Shortly thereafter, they make their first leadership blunder. It didn't involve the integration of two autonomous business units. It had nothing to do with how quality assurance related to process control.

The event centered around the denial of a simple request. No harm done, you thought? That is until you apply the age-old leadership measuring device, the Golden Rule, to the decision. Had the leader made the same request of his superior, he would have wanted the answer to be yes. Why did it happen? Hypocrisy? I don't think so. Ignorance? Maybe a little. Lack of leadership? Absolutely!

If you had to synthesize all the great works written on leadership into an eight-word sentence it would be "Treat others like you expect to be treated." When you violate the principle you stand a better chance of selling sand in the Sahara than leading at Mach 2.

How many times have you heard the statement "leaders are born, not made." I used to believe it. At the age of four, a gang of toddlers followed me around. I'd never taken any leadership classes, so it must have been in the genes. I held that opinion for a number of years. A lifetime of experience has taught me differently.

Genetics makes us what we are, but the range of possibilities as to what we can become is infinite. Functioning effectively as a leader has very little to do with IQ. Let's stop for a second. When I talk about leadership, I have a tendency to immediately think about history's great leaders: Napoleon Bonaparte, Frederick Douglass, Ralph Herrmanns, Clara Barton and Florence Nightingale.

These individuals are an exception, and circumstance is as much responsible for their names being on the tip of our tongues as their leadership ability. Had Saddam Hussein left Kuwait alone, Colin Powell's name would have less notoriety than the guy who ran the butcher shop at your local Safeway. In many cases, great leadership decisions are no different than lesser leadership decisions. William Stevenson once modestly stated, "There are no great men, there are only great events." Had Medio Waldt been sitting in Eisenhower's chair on June 5, 1944, and made the decision to invade Normandy, greatness probably would be attributed to him. Circumstance!

I'm not diminishing the roles these individuals played. It gives us all something to aspire to. I just don't want you to spend too much time thinking about them. I'd rather have you think about yourself. With the world population approaching six billion, you'll find there is more than enough to keep you busy.

I cannot think of any situation, in any environment, where leadership is not a prerequisite for success. You don't have to be Marvin Girouard, the president of Pier 1 imports, to make things better. As a matter of fact, his efforts would be futile if he couldn't mobilize leaders, in a thousand different areas, to participate in the process.

It's been said a journey of a thousand miles starts with an initial step, and the act of leading also has a beginning. Leading one impacts two and that affects four. The corresponding influence grows exponentially. All of a sudden, the process appears manageable. Before we lead the world, we can start with Bubba Applegate.

WALK! THEN RUN

In *Selling at Mach 1*, my basic premise centered around influence. To gain influence, I stated a salesman needed to make a positive impression on another person. Once that occurs the individual is more receptive to the message. Is leading others any different? Selling and leading both involve people, and the actions of the successful salesman and the effective leader in many cases coincide. Each gains influence through behavior. If behavior is fundamental to leadership, then the idea that leaders must be born starts to lose merit.

Impressions are formed through what people see. A leader's responsibility is to influence others. Others are influenced by behavior. Behavior is learned! People can be taught the behavior of leadership! Got it? Now we can pick up speed.

A long time before Taras Bulba redefined autocrat on the planes of Mongolia, leadership techniques had been examined under a microscope and critiqued by the experts. To this day, some authorities still believe mimicking the actions of history's icons is an effective way to lead others. If George Washington exhibited generosity, courage and determination, you should too. Or maybe you shouldn't.

I suspect if the father of our country and Julius Caesar ever compared notes on how each dealt with cowardice, there would be room for debate. There is just too much variability from situation to situation. In all my years of making leadership decisions I've never looked at anything from Hannibal's perspective, and you won't either.

IN THE BEGINNING

It happens quickly! One day you are classified as labor and then suddenly you aren't. "Worker bee" had nine letters. Leader has six. Make the right moves and you could get it down to four. Who wouldn't want to be the Boss. I guess a lot of people.

Some of the greatest leaders of our time have described their function as a cheerleader, coach, maitre d' and maestro. In contrast, some of the worst I've seen saw themselves as a warden, dictator or clearinghouse. They never figured it out. For them, leading meant "being in charge." Nothing could move forward until they blessed it. Top Dog meant you called the play.

Frankly, I have little concern for what happens to people who choose not to take the high road. From birth to death they'll probably be around seventy-five years, and how they fill the in between is up to them. I suspect the highlights of their career will come when they enter the rocking-chair phase of life. Sitting on the front porch, fantasies of greatness easily supplant acts of mediocrity.

If they existed in a vacuum there would be no need for *Leading at Mach 2*. Unfortunately they don't, and their actions impact upon us all. How many times have you been made unhappy by someone or something that did not meet your expectations? Your subsequent response, that holds them accountable, generates headlines everywhere: General Motors Experiences Record Losses, IBM in a Tailspin, XYZ Corporation Files Chapter 11.

The announcements are antiseptic. Words on paper cannot convey the human misery that is part and parcel of an organization that is failing. The finger pointing begins, excuses rain down and written analyses could fill the Love Canal. As Wall Street recoils and the search for a scapegoat begins, the Wosniaks find their name on the rolls of the unemployed.

Where did the problem begin? The genesis always occurred years before when someone else perpetuated a bad decision. R & D, systems integration, capital appropriation or some other abstruse activity becomes the culprit. Have you ever heard anyone confess, "Yes, I fiddled while my organization burned?"

AN AGE-OLD QUESTION

What do I do now? From supervisor of the night shift to president of the United States, leadership can be a frightening responsibility. Singular becomes plural, individual enterprise vanishes in the face of collective effort, and the welfare of the team supersedes all else.

Philosophy is great, but how do you turn an amorphous collection of leadership principles into reality. What actions on your part will make those you lead perform at a higher level.

Some facts might help you get started.

Did you know?

- People like to be led.

- They will decide who leads them.

- Their effort is a direct result of how they are treated.

Are you aware?

- Leaders adapt to individual needs.

- They do not treat everyone equally.

- Everyone is treated fairly.

It's undeniable! Trust is the adhesive that binds the two together.

TOMBSTONES DO TALK

Our chief want in life is somebody
who will make us do what we can.
— Ralph Waldo Emerson

Have you ever walked through a cemetery? The question is rhetorical. At one point in my life, when I was a twenty-two-year-old second lieutenant, I spent a great deal of time in cemeteries. It had nothing to do with being morbid, I just happened to be the Officer in Charge of several military funeral details. I actually liked the job.

I didn't care for the death part or seeing families in grief, but being involved in the last memory a person would have of their loved one seemed important. The Department of the Army thought so too. A senior officer would be sent to evaluate you and your honor guard's performance. Blow a funeral and you blew your career. Most officers were assigned the additional duty once a year, but because I volunteered to do it, I presented the flag at twenty-two ceremonies over a period of eighteen months.

Nothing about twenty-one-gun salutes, presenting the stars and stripes or having taps bring tears to your eyes has anything to do with *Leading at Mach 2*. Spending time at cemeteries does.

When you arrive at the burial site, you have time to pass, and nothing much to do except think about what will soon transpire and the part you play in it. Periodically, a tombstone catches your eye and you contemplate what its resident's life entailed before going to that final resting place.

On one particular scorching Georgia summer day, as I stood looking around, something struck me as peculiar. I had never seen such a dichotomy in the size and quality of the headstones in one cemetery. It appeared segregation played no part in the burial process. Everyone who died had access to a common plot of ground. There may have been chasms between them in life, but in death they were, in some instances, only inches apart. Big shot rested unceremoniously next to small fry.

The temperature did not allow for much further thought on the issue. We did our job and went home. Over time, the image of those tombstones kept surfacing in my mind. Initially, I attributed no significance to it. It had been just another funeral.

December 2, 1972, started pretty much like the day that preceded it. My platoon had just returned from our morning five-mile run and the troops were getting prepared for the day's activities.

As I walked through the orderly room door, the First Sergeant barked that the company commander wanted to see me. I entered his office and without hesitation he informed me he had just received a call from my branch officer at the Pentagon, and orders to Vietnam were forthcoming.

An opening had become available in the Military Assistance Command and I would be assigned as an advisor to a Vietnamese Armor Battalion. I had mixed emotions about the news. Because the war was winding down, I no longer thought of myself as a protector of democracy but I also knew my training had given me expertise in areas that were more suitable for combat than running a Seven Eleven. Vietnam and all its ancillary activity had been a part of my life since my father first went there in 1957. I looked forward to seeing it up close and personal.

Two days before my departure from Travis Air Force Base, Richard Nixon deprived me of the experience. His executive order mandated no more troops would be sent. New orders were cut and I traded in my jungle fatigues for a winter parka. Dong Du Chon, Korea, home of the Second Infantry Division, here I come.

I landed, reported in and awaited an assignment. In the interim, I functioned as a liaison officer between 8th Army and Division Headquarters. During a five-day operational readiness test, my job involved carrying communications between commanding generals and their subordinate commanders.

As the intermediary, I had a superficial involvement in the decision-making procedure. To describe it as an eye-opening experience would be an understatement. I found out very quickly that people in high places don't necessarily know what they are doing. The politics, pettiness, gamesmanship and, in some cases, downright stupidity was there for all, who were part of the inner sanctum, to see. In one instance, the gross mismanagement of a problem indicated to me the decision maker was not so much a commanding general as a general nuisance.

The war games came to an end and I rationalized it had been an aberrant situation. Somehow these people, these custodians of resources, these numskulls had slipped through the proverbial crack. They were in the minority. They had to be the exception.

A few days later, while standing at the bar in the officer's club, I overheard a brigade commander complaining about leadership in the division. He'd just relieved a company commander and waxed profusely about it. With one scotch in my belly and one in my hand, I decided I would partake in the conversation.

"It's not just the Second Infantry Division, sir. It's everywhere," I stated. He looked up, a little startled at my impertinence and interruption, and inquired, "Who are you, Lieutenant?" I told him. I could feel him sizing me up. My merit badges were making an impression. "Let's talk," he said. I couldn't wait to oblige and so we discussed it until the early hours.

Three days later I received a call inquiring whether I

would be interested in commanding Company A, 2nd S & T Battalion. I stated my MOS (Military Occupational Specialty) was combat arms not quartermaster, and I didn't think I held the proper qualifications. "F..k qualifications!" he quipped. "I've talked to the Division Commander and he's approved it. If you are a leader, you can command anything," he said.

His willingness to put an armor officer, not to mention a junior officer, in charge of the most critical operation in the division said something about Colonel Dick James. Leaders are risk takers and this action made a giant statement about him. The second I said "yes," his neck went into the noose. "I'll take it," I said. "You'll report to Battalion Headquarters on Monday," he replied.

Nothing I had previously done in my life had prepared me for what I would encounter. Alpha company had the mission to fulfill the 2nd Infantry Division's supply needs. There were clothing distribution warehouses, petroleum tank farms, food operations, barrier material and office equipment outlets, bath units, salvage yards, gas stations and a host of other supply related activities under its operational umbrella.

The company served customers from the DMZ in the north to the southern tip of Korea. Throw in a monstrous black market theft ring, an energy crisis and the worst racially charged environment in the Army, and you had a recipe for disaster. Shortly after I agreed to become the commander, I found out the company had just flunked the AGI (Annual General Inspection) and ranked last in the Division in most performance categories. Could I be in over my head? I thought so, but

I hadn't planned on making the army a career so I willingly accepted the challenge.

As I look back on the experience, I remember feeling a little intimated by what happened. I'd shot my mouth off and somebody called my hand. There I sat, twenty-four years old and the largest supply activity in Korea would be under my command. The problems were real, the environment hostile, and the interrelated nature of the operations made the mission complex.

In retrospect I shouldn't have worried about my qualifications. But, at the time, I didn't know leadership ability is a universal currency. It's accepted everywhere. I remember Colonel James telling me it was my show and he would stay out of it, but he wanted to see immediate results. When he said "immediate" a second time, I realized in two days I would leap from the frying pan into a towering inferno. I needed answers, and there was no time like the present to find them. Maybe history could help.

I reflected back on situations I'd read about, individuals who had motivated me and people I had led. The history books were filled with examples of leaders who made an immediate impact. They tapped into something their predecessor couldn't or wouldn't. The speed at which change came meant whatever they employed had been readily available. Because the triggering device lay at the surface, no major excavation was needed. Could it be that simple? Did a common thread run through every leadership challenge? I concluded the thread existed. The common denominator that determined success or failure centered around . . . People.

I tried to find an exception. What about the world of high technology? Computers were changing the landscape. No! Someone had to plug them in. I sat there for a few more hours and challenged the hypothesis. I finally accepted it.

For some reason my thoughts were teleported back to the cemetery in Georgia and the image of the grave markers. In death they were equals, but in life obviously there had been differences. I wondered if parallels could be drawn on a larger scale.

As I strained to come up with a plan of action, I experienced a flashback. Over the years I had tried to define leadership but something always seemed to be missing. Then one day as I turned a page in a book of quotes, it came to me like a thunderclap. My search for the Holy Grail ended.

> *"Leaders create energy in others*
> *by instilling purpose."*
> — *Unknown*

How could I have forgotten it. It made perfect sense. The tombstones were a physical representation of accomplishment. Accomplishment came from effort. Effort required energy.

ENERGY

- The work that a physical system is capable of doing in changing from its actual state to a specified reference state.

- Capacity for action or accomplishment.

- Strength and vigor.

Great organizations were filled with energy. Organizations in trouble were devoid of it. I reflected back on myriad experiences where I had seen excellence, mediocrity or failure, and energy had always been involved. Could it be that simple? Did leadership hinge on one word. Einstein thought so, $E=mc^2$. Energy is the essence of everything. Harness it and you become a master of the universe.

A PULL OF THE TRIGGER

I found out about energy the easy way. I had just assumed my first leadership position as a platoon leader in Company B 69th Armor and within hours of arriving I realized what the new volunteer Army was all about. The Department of Defense had lied. Bigger, stronger, faster and smarter. Who were they kidding? Each recruit individually selected—obviously from the unemployment line.

The following morning when I held my first formation it became immediately apparent my platoon consisted of the cast members from *Night of the Living*

Dead. I had a problem. Tank gunnery exercises were a month away and I would have to perform with thirty-one zombies. Energy, where were you? Two days later, it arrived unexpectedly on the firing range.

My platoon had gone to the range to qualify with the M-79 grenade launcher. For your information, the weapon looks similar to a sawed-off shotgun and can propel a highly explosive shell a considerable distance. It is classified as an indirect fire weapon because you don't point it directly at the target. You elevate the barrel and loft the projectile. It shoots like an artillery piece. Accuracy becomes a function of repetition and adjustment. Only those individuals who use the weapon regularly become good with it. I didn't fall in that category but my platoon didn't care. They had heard the exaggerated stories about Airborne Rangers and believed anyone that wore "The Tab" (a gold and black patch that says "Ranger" and signifies the wearer is Ranger qualified) could do anything.

As I arrived at the firing site, I was greeted by a chorus of "Come on Lieutenant, show us how." I hadn't planned on this. I was there to observe, not participate. I had a no-win situation. If I hit the tank hull 600 yards down range, a highly unlikely possibility, I would accomplish what they expected. If I missed it, they would judge me deficient. My credibility would be shot and Rangers around the world would want my scalp. There had to be a way out.

My exit strategy materialized quickly. "Get me a weapon, Platoon Sergeant," I commanded. I then instructed everyone to gather around. If I was going down, I would do it swinging. I talked about what they could demand from me and what I would expect from them. I defined cooperation, commitment, and what it felt like to be a winner.

The pep rally went on for about ten minutes and when my diatribe concluded there was nothing remaining but to fire the weapon. I walked up to the line as sixty-two eyes watched my every move. I looked down range and took a deep breath. I turned and said, "Men, any Ranger can hit that target ten out of ten times shooting the conventional way (my statement was nonsense). Let's make this challenging. I'm going to shoot it from my hip. If I don't hit the target, I buy the beer."

Nobody shoots an M-79 from the hip. If I missed I had an excuse: To try the impossible is admirable. To fail at it is understandable. I placed the weapon against my thigh, took every factor into account and pulled the trigger. Seven seconds later, an eruption of smoke blocked out the view of the target. It appeared I hit it dead center. From their perspective, I could have missed it by 100 yards and you wouldn't have known any different. I claimed a direct hit as thirty-one soldiers went crazy. I quickly jumped in my jeep and departed before they asked me for a repeat performance. As I looked back I realized, I had just learned something about energy.

SHOOT THE MOON

If you've never seen a rocket blast off, it's difficult to imagine the impact on your senses. To experience it at night enhances the visual affect. I happened to see two launchings during a three-month stay at Cocoa Beach, Florida. Even though my apartment lay about ten miles from the launch pad, when the rocket's boosters were ignited, the intense light and roar of the engines made you think the rocket left from your neighbor's lawn. Immediately you were engulfed in the event.

Your thoughts transcend time and place. The focus is upward and you can't help but wonder where it is going. You muse about other planets and civilizations. Then, as the rocket climbs inexorably onward and the brightness of its engines becomes but a pinhole of light in a shroud of blackness, you come back to your earthly senses.

Superlatives fill the air. Nobody has ever seen anything like it. The most awe inspiring concentrated release of energy I ever witnessed had been orchestrated by another person. I couldn't comprehend the incredible intellectual capacity needed by a rocket scientist to make a launch a reality.

While I sat in a classroom, geniuses assaulted the cosmos. I started to fantasize about the things I would accomplish if I had their brain. There would be no issue beyond my ken, no conflict too great to resolve. Suddenly, it dawned on me. Poverty, hatred, injustice, corruption, and a host of other social, political and economic malignancies could be found everywhere. Why hadn't the smart guys found a cure.

I knew the answer! I'd worked with a few rocket scientists over the years and they all suffered from the same affliction: control panel myopia. They had been programmed that the solution to every problem involved flipping a switch. When you did, it elicited a corresponding response. Only one possible reaction came from any given action. In rocket science, there were no alternatives. If the flight plan called for Mars, you didn't go to Venus.

Complications arise when you try to apply the same empirical methodology to issues involving human beings. The brain is not a computer, and man's physical and emotional evolution is a quantum leap backward from the evolution of technology. People are still killing each other. Greed, deceit, self-absorption and ignorance can be read about daily. Dinosaurs still exist! Reading the newspaper is proof positive.

Yes, technology has come light years from those cave days, but people haven't, and that's not all bad. It means we may not have to implement a program of "leadership du jour." The principles that motivated people three hundred years ago will work today and four hundred years from now. Not every aspect of our existence is caught in a maelstrom of change. The works of Socrates, Rembrandt and Beethoven are timeless in their ability to impact and influence. There is much that does not hinge on the introduction of a new microchip.

<u>N</u>OTES

CARRYING
THE LOAD

What's important, is not where
we are, but what direction
we are moving.
— *Oliver Wendell Holmes*

You've always wanted to lead, but up until now your success came vicariously through watching Roy Rogers movies. Don't be embarrassed. It's how a lot of people get started. In actuality, what you saw on the screen is pretty accurate as to how leaders operate. I'm not talking about their idiosyncratic differences. Superficially, Ben Franklin, Mohandas Gandhi and Charlemagne had nothing in common. But, beneath the surface, the leadership philosophy that dictated their behavior is identical. Roy knew right from wrong. He stood up for his beliefs, he cared about the people he led and he was prone to action. Who cares what saddle, rope or six-gun he used.

What matters is under his leadership something productive happened. Isn't that what leadership is about — taking a situation and making it better? Better is a relative term. It has no value until you apply the words, before and after.

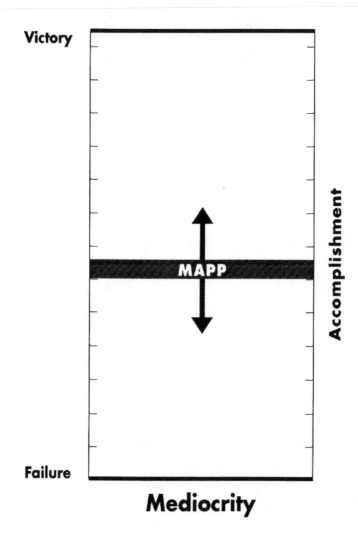

While a number of history's forgotten viewed the status quo as a comfort zone, Franklin Roosevelt, Robert Peary and Mark Rogers saw it as an anathema to human existence. I think most leaders do. Their view of success is not a point on a performance continuum. It is the distance traveled from where they began. Achievement is a function of many things, none more important than the standards you set up front. I believe it starts with the Spectrum of Accomplishment.

What you are looking at is nothing more than a vertical scale that reflects a range of activity. At one end you have Victory at the other Failure. In addition, somewhere on the scale, there is a dividing point between the two extremes. We will identify it as the MAPP (Minimum Acceptable Performance Point).

Average leaders accept the position of the MAPP as equal distance between Victory and Failure. They reject self-determination and believe you have to take the good with the bad. Performance is linked to fate and whatever comes your way must be accepted. Their attitude creates an environment where the participants never rise above mediocrity.

Nonleaders have a different approach. They push the MAPP to a level where everyone can meet it. No matter how minimal the effort, you still qualify. Is it any wonder their organizations don't achieve anything. Meeting the minimum is not only one step away from failure, but also a quantum leap from victory. Everywhere you look people are struggling, frustrated and dissatisfied.

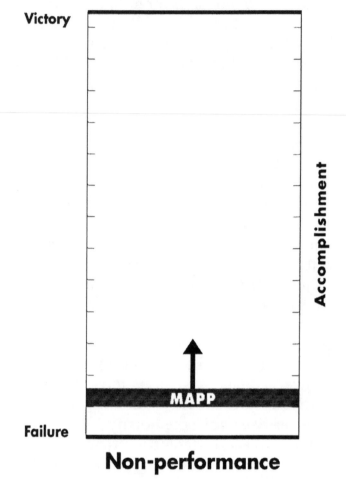

Non-performance

Individuals who lead at Mach 2 recognize elevating the MAPP is crucial to consistent performance. In looking at their Spectrum of Accomplishment, the Minimum Acceptable Performance Point is almost indistinguishable from the Victory point. When their people meet the lowest requirement, they are in position to win. If they fall beneath the standard they are probably still a long way from failure.

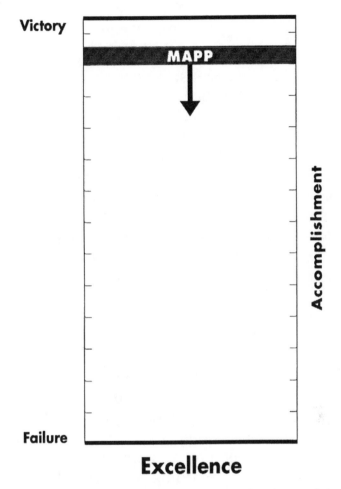

Excellence

Do you think MAPP placement had anything to do with Vince Lombardi taking a group of substandard performers to NFL greatness. I think that's how leadership and coaching became associated. Is there any difference between placement of the MAPP on the field of battle or the pole-vault pit? Ask Dan O'Brien.

HE DID WHAT?

There are many Madison Avenue stories that surround world championships, but none took on the significance of the battle between Dave and Dan, the world's two best decathletes in the 1988 Olympics. Reebok, the giant apparel company had spent millions of dollars promoting the competition between these two world champions. The build-up started months before, and a tremendous amount of human interest had been generated around the competition.

The odds makers in Las Vegas gave the edge to Dan because he held the world title and in his most recent encounters with Dave, he came out victorious. The world awaited the clash between these two titans of track and field. What had been billed as *the* competition of the Seoul games came to a screeching halt at the Olympic trials.

It shouldn't have happened, but Dan and his coach didn't understand that the Minimum Acceptable Performance Point lives in a dynamic state. It slides up or down based upon a variety of factors. The object is to meet the MAPP. Depending upon the ease with which you do it, you adjust accordingly. On this day Dan's systems were a little slow in getting up to speed. Who knows why, but he decided to pass on the first four MAPPs. He must have been thinking he would save energy by starting with the fifth MAPP 15'9". In practice he easily cleared that height. It wouldn't be a problem, or so he thought. Three attempts later, his Olympic aspirations came to an end.

Is performance merely a function of MAPP placement. Some leaders think so. They choose Pythagoras over Freud. Set the standard, demand compliance, and results are sure to follow. We're all familiar with the case studies: Bligh and the Bounty, Custer at Little Big Horn, and Johnson at Acme Inc. If you sat down and broke bread with some of history's worst, you would find they weren't devils. They were just ignorant.

Had they studied under Tom Costello, president of ResourceNet International, they would have learned that leading others involves nondeterministic humanism. There is no empirical standard. MAPPS are established based upon an individual's ability to perform.

What Angela, the All-American MBA from Harvard, will accept as her MAPP might be dramatically different from Walt, the high school dropout, will accept as his. Is it any wonder that when leaders indulge in MAPPing their organization the Spectrum of Accomplishment looks like a ladder.

Do you think you are going to accomplish anything if your followers aren't in agreement? Ask Frank Lorenzo, the despised former CEO of the now defunct Eastern Airlines, what he thinks.

What is it that makes another person stand up and say, "I'm with you," and then perform. Not all that much! The difficulty arises when you don't understand your role. Your responsibility as a leader is to get people to respond, by helping them achieve their goals.

When you do, they will want to keep you around. Volumes have been written on the subject, but when you distill out all the extraneous filler, it boils down to this: When you help me, I'll help you, and together we will get something done.

Is it any more complicated than that? John Akers, the former chairman of IBM, thought so. The analysis of his ride into the Hall of Shame could fill a library, but I can sum it up with one word, **COMBUSTION**, or lack of it. He should have taken a course in petroleum engineering. If he had, he'd occupy a different place in business history.

In 1974 I spent four months at the U.S. Petroleum Institute. While there, I learned about the various petroleum distillates that are produced in a cracking tower, when refining a barrel of crude oil. At varying temperatures, different products appear. I'm sure you are familiar with the names: diesel fuel, gasoline, kerosene and alcohol to name a few.

Each has its own chemical composition and ability to provide energy. Here comes the curve ball. Different engines require different fuels. What propels a Sheridan assault vehicle will ground a helicopter. The fuel that enables an aircraft carrier to cruise at twenty knots will flatten a jeep. In addition, because of their physical characteristics, each one, ignites at a different temperature. Even that will vary, based upon a variety of environmental factors.

Now the guys who produce petroleum products are pretty smart, so they color each distillate differently. They want you to match the right fuel with its compatible engine. When that happens, ignition takes place. You can have the most sophisticated hardware in the world but if you can't get it running you have nothing. Had John Akers been to petroleum school he would have understood, without combustion, tanks never leave the motor pool.

Do you think I'm being a little hard on him. I call it justice. If you are going to accept the salary, perks and recognition of being Numero Uno, you should be held accountable for what happens on your watch.

I would think he is now questioning why, under his leadership, the organization failed. If he listens to his inner voice, he will never understand it. Bureaucratic intervention, unionization, environmental restrictions, legal entanglements and economic downturns are ego-driven rationalizations for arrogance, dissension, exclusion, ineptitude and constraint.

John and a number of those individuals he kept in responsible positions didn't realize their actions would be the fuel that drove the organizational engine, or should we make that plural?

Every organization is an amalgamation of engines. Each one individually assembled with a capability to perform a specific function. In the pits of Indianapolis they go by Chevy, Ford, Ferrari and Porsche, but in most environments they're called Jane, Bob, Linda and Joan. What gets them up and going has nothing to do with an octane rating. The horsepower they generate will be a direct result of their leader's behavior.

Many years ago, I held the view that leadership meant strength. All my actions were measured against that criterion. I went out of my way to be visible, aggressive, outspoken and tough in everything I did. In retrospect, I believe my actions were the result of a misunderstanding that leaders need to intimidate.

Experience has given me a different perspective. I have now come to the realization that another human being's willingness to respond to me, as their leader, is in large part a direct result of how they view the integrity of the relationship.

INTEGRITY

- Moral or ethical strength.

- The condition of being free from defects.

- A state of being entirely whole.

- The quality of being honest.

I'll add a few more: thoughtful, kind, concerned and compassionate. I could go on, but I'm not as interested with its definitive interpretation as I am with operational significance. Without integrity there will be no loyalty.

LOYALTY

- Steadfast in allegiance.

- Faithful to a person, ideal or custom.

Are you going to commit to someone you don't trust? Loyalty is the intangible underpinning that anchors relationships. When loyalty is present, an impenetrable energy source is created that protects the organization. Leaders that place a high premium on building loyalty, create environments where membership lasts for life. When individuals are loyal they make commitments that often defy reason. Their conscience gives them no other choice. Death becomes preferable to betrayal.

I've never met a leader of any consequence who didn't take great pride in the loyalty they built in their organization. Ask any hundred leaders what five attributes reflect an organization's health and I would be surprised if all of them didn't include loyalty.

AN EMOTIONAL SUBJECT

Two years ago I received a résumé from a young captain who had made the decision to leave the Army and pursue a civilian career. I didn't have any positions available but his résumé and cover letter so impressed me, I decided to meet with him to discuss his future. In the course of our conversation, I asked him for his definition of leadership. I could see my question had an impact.

When leaders are asked about the subject, their response is normally a product of experience. Apparently, Derek Van Johnson, an African-American graduate of West Point, had some strong feelings on the issue. As one of the Army's most highly trained combat infantrymen, Derek and his unit had led the United States assault into Panama. It had been a life and death experience and only he and his men could appreciate the bond between them. He gave a quick answer and we moved on to another subject. Two days later, it became apparent he had not been satisfied with his reply.

Dear Steve,

After you left the other night I returned home and thought about my comments on leadership. The subject deserves more than a forty second response, so I thought I would put my feelings in writing.
LEADERSHIP IS COMMITMENT!!
Someone once relayed an analogy to me about commitment. The reference was to a breakfast meal consisting of bacon and eggs. In this scenario, the hen is a contributor, but the pig is COMMITTED. *The discussion focused on the definition of true commitment. In its purest sense, commitment requires total dedication of an asset, ability, attitude and action. Taken to the extreme sacrifice, as in the pig's case, commitment is measured by a person's willingness to die for a cause or concern.*

I believe that commitment consists of demonstrated love and loyalty. I do not mean the kind of melancholy and sentimentalism of porch swings and long walks with someone special. Nor do I describe the "one-way" loyalty prevalent in many organizational structures. The love I refer to is the kind of joint, collective dedication to something beyond your individual capability or capacity. The loyalty I mention here is never spoken. This loyalty resides in the minds and hearts of teams of men and women with individual strengths and complementary weaknesses. This loyalty resists categorization because of its mutual, unwavering and voluntarily shared responsibility for its maintenance.

During the period of March 1989 to May 1990, I enjoyed the privilege of commanding an Airborne Rifle Company in the 82nd Airborne Division at Ft. Bragg, North Carolina. The distinct honor of this opportunity carried an additional burden of my predecessor's success and the overall outstanding combat readiness of the company. How could I carry on? What could I do to make this good organization better? The answers were inside me and locked within the individual talents of the soldiers. I learned about approach, motivation, loyalty, common sense and common ground (both literal and figurative). I learned that, together, we could optimize these aspects of the organization.

Collectively, the company was an outstanding unit. However, individual talents had not been nurtured or exploited for their synergistic effects. Tapping into reservoirs of skill, aspiration and experience would prove to be the catalysts to even greater accomplishments. By sharing and cross-fertilizing knowledge and techniques, by challenging with leadership those who had only previously known how to follow, the company's ability to execute under duress and austere conditions flourished.

On the night of December 19, 1989, my company was about to conduct a nighttime, air assault/ waterborne, combat attack on the Renacer Prison near Gamboa, Panama, in support of Operation Just Cause. The success of the mission (five enemy KIA, twenty-two captured, sixty-four political prisoners secured, one friendly casualty) is not the most important issue. Everything that had led up to this event is what enabled the company to be as effective as we were. We sweat and bled together on road marches and tactical exercises. We collectively cheated death during mass tactical parachute assaults. We destroyed our sister companies on the athletic fields and the parade field. We developed a fierce, territorial pride, to a cause greater than our individual interests.

But, we would not have been able to have been this effective without the familial love (spelled c-o-m-m-i-t-m-e-n-t) for what we were doing. Every day there were conflicts and hard choices to make. But again, always, there was a unity of purpose. We shared, to a man, every hardship, every triumph, every rehearsal, every loss equally. We built a genuine respect and reverence for one another and for the Company. Leadership — personal, common sense, direct and honest leadership — made this series of successes possible. But this was not my leadership. It was the leadership of SPC Schleben who earned a Bronze Star with "V" Device for his heroic actions the morning of December 20, 1989. It was the leadership of PFC Mays, labeled a "bad" soldier before the company took a chance and challenged his leadership ability. There were soldiers like 1Lt. Stephen Galloway, who taught me that leadership is first and foremost internal, that it is not about words, but decisive, correct and effective action. Leadership enabled the men of "Coldsteel Charlie" Company to be patient and willing to listen to me after I demonstrated the ability to listen to them.

That night, just before I ordered the company into combat, I reviewed what we were about to do. I told them we were all coming back alive and that I loved them. Though it was pitch black and I could see no faces, I could feel their steely resolve and the spirit of thousands more. There was nothing left to say. I knew that we would lead one another through this challenge, and through leadership, we were committed.

Sincerely,

Derek

Footnote: Captain Van Johnson also received the Bronze Star medal for his leadership that night.

I suspect I will keep his letter for the rest of my life and read it many more times. The inspiration comes not so much from what Derek writes, as it does from the passion that forced him to set the record straight. Here is an individual who comprehends the essence of leadership and is incapable of keeping it to himself.

Derek, you lead and I'll follow.

REMOVE THOSE CUFFS

There are two ways of exerting one's strength: pushing down or pulling up.
— *Booker T. Washington*

As important as building loyalty is to the process of getting something accomplished, it is only part of the equation. Loyalty in and of itself has little worth. What did the residents of Jonestown accomplish? How about the zealots who followed Maharishi Micki Moto? Did you think those guys were leaders? When an individual dominates another person, it's for one reason . . . self-interest. They can't be leaders because leadership is about looking out for someone else. It means you are prepared to sacrifice your interests on behalf of others.

Energy! How important is it? A couple of clichés may help us out: *lying down on the job* or *up and run-*

ning. One conjures up images of nonperformance while the other elicits a view of action. Can action exist without effort? Is effort possible without energy?

A.K.A. SUSHI MAN

If I mentioned the name W. Edwards Deming would a bell go off? Do you attribute your knowledge of how to spell Toyota to this statistician from Wyoming? You should. He is given primary credit for making Japan the industrial powerhouse it is today. Shortly after World War II, Deming showed up on the emperor's doorstep and stated he had a plan that would turn Japan from the laughingstock of industrial producers to the most respected performance-driven country on earth. The entire program could be spelled in twenty-five letters: Statistical Process Control.

His concept and resulting implementation focused on reducing variability in processes. He concluded that only by keeping track of the variance between a prescribed goal and an end result could you make adjustments to better the process and insure consistency. Statistics were the empirical tool that took subjectivity out of the equation. Reduce variance and you would improve quality. The corresponding success of Deming's methods and universal acceptance are proof positive he knew his stuff.

The nature of leading others is less empirical, but Deming's thoughts on reducing variance do apply. I'm not talking about the statistics that are part and parcel of any well-run organization. There are enough rocket scientists around to keep track of them.

I'm concerned with variance, but spread sheets are

only part of the answer. Each number or body of data also has a person behind it. I want to know what is going on inside her mind. What does she need to perform at a higher level? Does he lack education, commitment or authority? Is their freedom of movement inhibited? Do they need help? Why aren't they responsive? These basic questions have answers. Numbers can't talk, but people are dying to.

I never had any doubts most of the rocket scientists I've replaced were smarter than me. They just had trouble identifying what held real relevance to getting something done. In retrospect, I can't remember one who oriented downward. Their concern always hinged on the view they projected to those above. They failed to recognize the energy resided below. For every queen bee there were a thousand worker bees.

WHAT DEODORANT DO YOU USE?

A few years ago, a deodorant commercial depicted an actor playing basketball and then walking briskly off the court. As he faced the camera with a modicum of sweat, he stated, "I give a 110 percent and I expect a 110 percent from everybody and everything." He then quickly showered, applied the deodorant that gave him what he demanded and headed for his date.

Two things immediately came to mind. The guy suffered from stupidity or he happened to be a moonlighting politician who thought fiction got more votes than fact. Wake up buster. Nobody gives 110 percent. In fact, you won't find anybody who gives a hundred percent. When you've given everything, your next stop is the cemetery.

You might as well face it. Your best people operate at 60 to 70 percent and your worst are at 15 to 20. You don't need a calculator to figure there is considerable upward potential.

THE SKIES OVER MIAMI

There were lots of things going on in 1981, but I'm only concerned with what happened at the Federal Aviation Administration. The air traffic controllers were unhappy with their work conditions and threatened to go on strike. Nobody would argue that being an ATC wasn't one of the most intense, pressure-filled jobs in America. As a whole, the group exhibited high rates of burnout, divorce and suicide.

The job was tough! During the time they were on duty they operated as close to capacity as any white collar worker in the country. Their strike declaration stated they couldn't do any more and if conditions didn't improve, they would walk. Ronald Reagan rejected their demands and they did. Their leaders made a major miscalculation. Virtually, the entire group was replaced . . .with half as many people. Did planes crash all over America? I think you know the answer.

Deming tells us performance involves reducing variability and Einstein says energy is a catalyst for everything. It appears we're rolling but we still haven't addressed the issue of purpose. "Leaders create energy in others by instilling *purpose.*" Apparently, it is crucial to the equation. But what is it? Psychologists have tried to define the term for decades. Freud, Jung, and Skinner all had their thoughts on the subject. Whether we call it self-gratification, motivation, need satisfaction or some other name, it all boils down to the impetus that makes each of us perform.

In 1957 Abraham Harold Maslow came up with a behavioral model that focused on a hierarchy of needs. It looked much like a pyramid consisting of various layers. The model depicted the order in which needs were prioritized. Maslow's accompanying analysis stated people did not focus on higher level desires until lower level ones had been fulfilled. At the time, food, clothing, shelter and security were the hierarchy's major areas of consideration.

If Maslow created the model today, it would look a bit different. Survival is no longer predicated on one's ability to fulfill basic needs. Food, clothing and shelter are a given. Acceptance, involvement, reward and recognition have replaced them. Instilling purpose requires a different orientation. The circa 2000 behavioral model places greater emphasis on feeding the brain than the belly.

A STATE OF MIND

You don't have to be a psychiatrist to understand the power the mind has over the body. Ask a manic depressive. Physically nothing changes, but emotionally something is activated in the brain that inhibits the process of turning thought into action. If you plotted the manic depressive's output on a Physical Activity Chart and connected the points, you would have two parallel lines. Manic depression is the behavior of extremes. In the manic phase, the energy is difficult to contain. Enthusiasm and insight give rise to energy that transcends human understanding. How did van Gogh, Keats, Byron and Shelley accomplish so much? During the depressive stage it manifests itself as paralysis. Getting out of bed becomes a monumental challenge.

Thanks to medical science, chemistry now provides a remedy that limits the emotional range. Treatment for the disorder seeks a middle ground. The manic depressive is deprived of the exhilarating, productive high but also is spared the demoralizing, incapacitating low. On balance, these individuals lives become livable, but only through compromise.

What does manic depression have to do with leadership? Nothing. I brought the subject up merely to illustrate the point, that the driving force behind action is primarily psychological. If the brain is willing, the body will follow. There has never been a leader of any consequence that didn't understand the concept. Winston Churchill was a master psychologist. One thirty-minute speech filled with a potpourri of Churchillisms and you couldn't wait to jump into the fray; so what if it might cost you your life.

In contrast, not a day goes by where you don't encounter someone who is being poorly lead. Given a choice of right or wrong, good or bad, up or down, they seem to always choose what's most expedient. They continually make unilateral decisions to give less.

Are they to blame or are they just another victim of poor leadership? The paper trail may go back as far as childhood, where they were deprived of parental leadership, or it may start with their present supervisor. Whatever the case, because they don't operate in a vacuum we all suffer the consequences of their nonperformance. That's the bad news. The good news is it doesn't have to happen.

AN OUNCE OF PREVENTION

If you aren't familiar with Theory X — Theory Y management style, let me enlighten you. Theory X managers think people are inherently bad and must be dominated if you are going to accomplish anything. Theory Y proponents hold the opposite view. They believe people have great worth and their inner drive yearns for the opportunity to excel. When given a choice between right or wrong, they instinctively choose the former. All they need is an environment that encourages their natural inclination.

X is about control. Y focuses on support. I would guess if you surveyed a group of leaders from failing organizations, held up both cards and asked them to pick the one that approximates their style, not one in the crowd would choose the X. Its management tenets have been proven obsolete and only a dummy would support them. That's good news also. It shows, at least philosophically, they are in sync with modern day theory. Now the bad news. Talk is cheap and what they profess as their leadership style in no way shows up on the videotape. Why does it happen? I'll give you three reasons:

- **Ignorance:** They may be a victim also. When they were trying to find their way as a leader they were given no help. Their actions are now a product of a leadership mind-set connected to a patchwork of archaic experiences. They haven't figured out that what worked in the past may not be appropriate today.

- **Apathy:** A curse that comes with being uninvolved. Commitment takes effort. Lots of people are happy to be spectators. They don't understand involvement leads to development. Sitting on the sidelines results in physical and psychological atrophy. It's no surprise when it's time to play ball, they can't get off the bench.

- **Cowardice:** Standing up for what you believe in will put you in confrontation with others. Confrontation involves risk and there are many who avoid it. They fail to recognize without the support that backbone provides, the entire structure will collapse.

Do you show some of the symptoms? It's not fatal. The remedy for ignorance is knowledge. Shifting into gear will distance you from apathy, and if you don't tell anyone you are a coward, they might never find out. It's a fact that a number of recognizable leaders were cowards. They came up short on courage, but because they did enough of the right things in other areas, their battles were always fought for them.

IN SHEEP'S
CLOTHING

Injustice anywhere is a threat
to justice everywhere.
— Martin Luther King, Jr.

I never met Robert Oppenheimer, but I know we share one view in common. We both understand how critical the environment is to producing energy. Had he not been so diligent at keeping impurities out of the atomic lab, Los Alamos would be known for tumbleweeds and sand dunes.

I've found most leaders understand the harmful effects of contamination. Have you ever watched one in action. There is no huffing and puffing, no threats of "I'll blow your house down." Very seldom do they exhibit an "in your face" strategy. Their program has been implemented and they are now awaiting the results that are sure to follow.

Suddenly, something gets their attention. Senses come alive! A breach of security has been detected. Immediately, they identify whether the intrusion is innocuous or a threat. If it's the latter, their attack is swift and ferocious. It has only one objective and that is to remove the foreign presence. Their actions are not the result of a samurai mentality. They are just protective of the environment they created.

IN SEARCH OF TURKEYS

It didn't make the front page of the *Wall Street Journal*, but in Korea in the fall of 1973, the hottest news to hit the country since the Korean armistice, would play out on Thanksgiving Day.

It had nothing to do with the peace talks between the two Koreas. This event centered around turkeys. The new division commander, General Henry K. Emerson, "The Gunfighter," a legendary Vietnam hero, had made the decision to feed his troops fresh whole turkeys for the occasion. The previous two decades everyone had eaten a processed substitute, so this was a major departure from the norm. The troops were ecstatic.

My company would have the responsibility of procuring, refrigerating and distributing the turkeys. I had become fairly adept at identifying potential theft opportunities, but in my greatest suspicions I couldn't imagine the ever-bold Korean black market targeting this highly visible event. I was wrong. Luckily the military's Criminal Investigation Division had gotten wind of the plot and arrived to make arrests and save the unfeathered fowl.

While the drama played out, the birds were delayed in getting to the distribution point. When the individual units arrived to receive their gobblers and found they weren't available, word swept like a brush fire that the turkey deal was a hoax. Within minutes of hearing about the problem, the Assistant Division Commander (ADC) was in my company area berating my subsistence section.

When I received the call at company headquarters, my career flashed in front of my eyes. Not because of the turkey dilemma, but rather the confrontation that was about to ensue.

At issue was a fundamental tenet of leadership: The Chain of Command. These people were my responsibility and now they were being abused by someone who had nothing to do with them.

As I ran out of the Quonset hut, my first sergeant followed in hot pursuit. I could see the ADC in the distance pointing his finger at one of my men. I had no options. If I let him continue, it would destroy the perception, when you worked for me, you were accountable, only to me. Now I had an interloper screwing up a delicate situation.

When I reached the general, I was surprised the officer in charge, a former Clemson linebacker, hadn't taken him on. It must have been due to his respect for my chain of command. He knew I'd want first shot.

I'm hot tempered but I'm not stupid. I had no idea how this would play out, but I knew if I showed proper military courtesy, I would be in a better position to ask for clemency at my court-martial.

When I got to him, his greeting was anything but

cordial. Ten epithets later he asked for my response. "Sir, you are in violation of the chain of command (I knew The Gunfighter embraced the concept) and I would like you to leave my company area, sir." I said nothing else and waited for his scathing reply. He stood in silence for what seemed an interminably long time, about five seconds, and then his only response, was to direct his driver to start the jeep and take him back to division headquarters.

It turned out he hadn't achieved his rank by accident. As a result, he understood the bond between leader and follower is sacred. A temporary lapse, due to "turkeystances" beyond his control, had gotten the best of him. When he had a moment to reflect on my comment, he recognized the error of his ways.

The turkeys arrived a few hours later, the troops of the Division had a joyous T-day, and I never heard another word on the subject.

Unfortunately, examples like the above are not unique. I think that's why so many leaders take on the additional role of sanitation engineer. In a perfect world, processes are allowed to realize their potential unencumbered. In our flawed existence, everyone wants to mess with your experiment.

You don't have to allow it to happen. I won't! It's not that I'm a fatalist, masochist or obstructionist. I just know when pollution infiltrates an organization, people's ability to perform is impacted. Ten parts plutonium with one part contamination, and a nuclear reaction becomes a nuclear fizzle. When the environment is right, energy is created, and when something is wrong, energy is lost.

RIGHT? WRONG?

We're not dealing with cosmic secrets. Leadership means creating energy in others. Your actions as their leader will either start their engine, or turn it off. If

UNIVERSAL ENERGY CHART

CONTAMINATION		COMBUSTION	
Incapacitator	Depletor	Enhancer	Energizer
Abuse	Insensitivity	Courtesy	Freedom
Betrayal	Ambiguity	Sensitivity	Authority
Deceit	Ambivalence	Kindness	Confidence
Control	Apathy	Inclusion	Trust
Castigation	Pettiness	Cooperation	Courage
Humiliation	Pessimism	Consideration	Generosity
Embarrassment	Ignorance	Involvement	Passion
Cowardice	Neglect	Recognition	Praise
Oppression	Myopia	Acceptance	Decisiveness

that's the case then I think it's important we identify some combustible as well as contaminating behavior.

The matrix is self-explanatory. In my mind, your behavior is either productive or unproductive. In that certain actions elicit a greater or lesser response, I've created four categories of activity. **Energizers** describe actions that have a dramatic, uplifting effect (a promotion). **Enhancers** move a situation forward but at a slower pace (a letter of appreciation). **Depletors** send energy into hibernation (a reprimand), while **Incapacitators** will absolutely destroy a relationship (public condemnation).

Energy! When people have it they are able to respond to the task at hand. All of a sudden, putting your finger in the dike, resolving a customer complaint or repulsing an enemy attack becomes a piece of cake.

The question becomes, where should we concentrate our effort? In a world as complex as the one in which we exist, if we can't distinguish what is significant from what is mundane, we will spend a lot of time chasing our tails.

My experience has taught me focusing on less is better. When you concentrate on everything, you accomplish nothing. It should come as no surprise not every issue needs a leader's attention. People have an incredible capacity to overcome their own problems. In many cases by working through organizational irritants they become stronger. Activity builds fitness.

Wasn't that Jonas Salk's strategy? Let a few germs in and build up an immune system. It took me a few years to figure it out, but now I don't sweat the small stuff. I no longer worry about Sonja punching in late,

Bruno taking the day off or Hank putting $12.50 on his expense account. If it doesn't have an impact on the creation or depletion of energy, I leave it alone.

It's easy to say, but if you've never been in garbage disposal, identifying contaminants can be a problem. Not everything that smells bad and looks like toxic waste is harmful, and just because it's dressed like innocent Little Red Riding Hood doesn't mean it won't eat you alive.

I NEVER MET A MEETING I LIKED

It hurts me to say that, because in my youth I had a different view. *The American Heritage Dictionary* states a meeting is a place where things join, a coming together, an assembly. What could be better? Bring people into a public forum and let their fertile minds solve the issues of the day. I've never questioned that the collective wisdom of a group far exceeds that of any one member. It just makes sense to get everyone involved.

A quick look back in history reinforces the concept. Without a meeting the Declaration of Independence would never have been written, Yalta would be known for fish, and the Lewis and Clark Expedition would have ended in St. Louis. Over the centuries meetings have served mankind as a forum for intellectual discourse.

As I'm writing this, I'm starting to experience cognitive dissonance. Although, I've been enlightened by hundreds of literary works where great minds came together, I have suffered mightily at the hands of individuals who requested I attend their meeting. Sitting in a chair, locked in a room, observing the incessant posturing of the meeting participants, oftentimes I wished God would take me right then and there.

I have nothing against the concept of meeting per se. People on occasion need to meet to discuss things. It is a necessary evil. The problem arises when some authority thinks that meetings are a sine qua non of organizational existence. Let me explain why they aren't.

If you analyzed the purpose of a meeting in the abstract it would be difficult to find fault with why they exist. Meetings aren't held to waste people's time, squander resources and remove decision makers from their daily responsibilities. But, that's exactly what happens. The ideas that underlie the purpose of holding a meeting are noble. The reality of what transpires in most meetings belies the original objective.

SOME FACTS ABOUT MEETINGS

- There are too many.

Nothing is resolved in the contemplative stage of management. Resolution comes from implementation, and I have never seen anything implemented in a meeting room. Is it any wonder organizations that seem to be having the greatest problems meet the most. Decision makers are never available. On the other hand, I've found when I call a manager at a successful company, more often than not, the individual is waiting for my call.

- They're too long.

On any given issue there are only a few factors that have any real importance. The rest is minutiae that, for a number of reasons, gets injected into the discussion. Participants feel a need to state their thoughts on everything and with each elocution the meeting is extended. People become bored and dispirited, and exit the activity in an enervated state. Many of the critical issues get buried in the manure.

- Participants are at cross-purposes.

Everyone has their own agenda. Whenever you bring people together, you give them an opportunity to act on those agendas. Meetings are a great place to perform in front of peers, subordinates and superiors. Altruism is supplanted by career positioning. Most participants show up with a desire to hear what is presented and speak if they have something to say. The Bully, Squirrel and Intellectual come for different reasons.

THE BULLY

Dominating behavior stems from insecurity and its aggressive nature is a cover-up for doubts about self-worth and other perceived or real shortcomings. Bullies use meetings to project and reinforce their authoritative image. Their overbearing behavior inhibits openness and honesty and will greatly diminish the quality of any forum. For them, meetings are a narcotic and they need a regular fix.

THE SQUIRREL

The squirrel suffers from the same insecurity as the bully but the manifestation is different. Squirrels love the opportunity to associate with others. In their never-ending quest to find sponsorship they support everyone's view. No decision can be made because everyone has an excellent point.

THE INTELLECTUAL

This individual is so smart it hurts. Carrying the burden of genius is a curse. Relief comes only from sharing insight with others. Meetings are a great place to enlighten many at once. The intellectual finds it impossible not to express his or her view on every conceivable issue. They understand the upside, the downside and all sides in between. The meeting is running two hours over and they are just getting warmed up.

- Meetings are poorly managed.

Each has its own objective, and how it is managed will determine its value and success. In no way should you view a meeting as a democratic forum. Meetings, if they must be held, serve one purpose and that is to accomplish the agenda. The sooner the better. Whoever has the responsibility for the meeting is a benevolent dictator at best and if things start to deteriorate the transformation to autocrat needs to be swift. Tyranny is preferential to anarchy.

Holding productive meetings is not difficult if you understand the rules:

The meeting is the leader's responsibility.
Everyone must stick to the facts.
Editorial comments are off-limits.
Too little is always better than too much.
Meetings must start and end on time.

I've always been amazed at the importance some people place on meetings. The facts prove differently. The vast majority of people I've known hate meetings. I think I know why. People who excel are prone to action. They are intimately involved with their operation and their focus is on responsiveness to employees and customers. Trapped in a room behind closed doors, they can respond to nothing. Is it any wonder they are impatient to conclude the event. Individuals that are less successful are less involved, and find great joy in sharing thoughts and eating danish.

SIMPLE MATHEMATICS

A decade ago I did a study on why a business unit of International Paper had trouble meeting its sales objectives. In that I had responsibility for the group, I thought a way to secure my future employment would be to resolve the issue. A quick analysis illuminated the problem.

For salespeople to be effective, they need to be in front of customers. There is a direct correlation between customer interaction and success. The question then became, how much time did the sales reps actually spend with buyers. I surveyed them and their response indicated, far too little. The majority stated they were always in meetings.

I had a presentation coming up at an executive conference and I decided to deliver the message there. A simple chart accurately showed the problem.

The numbers were rounded off or averaged to simplify the picture, but the fact still remained, in the

TOTAL DAYS IN A YEAR	365
Less	
Holidays	17
Vacation days	14
Weekends	104
Administrative days	80
Sick days	7
Travel	50
Meetings	63
DAYS LEFT FOR SELLING	**30**

course of a year the sales reps did not spend a great deal of time selling. They were burdened in many cases with activities that generated no profit for the corporation.

I couldn't do anything about travel. Technology didn't allow for Scotty to beam them around. The administrative burden came from the chairman's office, and carried executive immunity. Meetings though, were fair game. One of my first acts canceled weekly regional meetings. With one conference call, I more than doubled the time they had to sell. The corresponding success of the business group indicated my decision had been correct.

SAY IT AIN'T SO JOE

Let me qualify what I said about the antipathy generated by meetings. In my mind there are three types:

informational, issue resolution, recreational. People tend to only dislike the first two.

Who doesn't want to have fun? The reason behind holding a recreational meeting is to let your team rest and recuperate from the demands your leadership places upon them. The more dedicated the individual, the tougher it is to leave the job at the office. Thinking about your responsibilities can be as enervating as performing them. Being conscientious takes its toll. Enter, the recreational meeting. The objective is to remove people from the work environment so they can recharge their batteries.

Leaders who understand the reasons behind a recreational meeting make it: an event. Even though the cost of holding the meeting is high, the payback is enormous. Building a team requires professional as well as personal interaction. At recreational meetings relationships are built, bodies energized and memories of the camaraderie made long lasting. People leave the meeting knowing their leader appreciates their effort. After three days of eating oysters the size of footballs, they return to work, ready to go to war.

The concept shouldn't be hard to understand or maybe it is. A few years ago I accepted an invitation to speak at the fiftieth anniversary of a highly successful corporation. When I showed up at the cocktail party, I couldn't believe my eyes. People had literally traveled from around the globe to be greeted by an hors d'oeuvres table consisting of peanuts, potato chips and popcorn. If you wanted to wash the sodium down with a beverage, you had the option of soda pop, jug wine or beer.

What could the meeting organizer have been thinking. "If it looks like a boondoggle, smells like a boondoggle, but doesn't taste like one, I will have fooled them?" As interesting as that logic may be, it isn't novel. Joe W. rewarded his organization for their outstanding performance by holding the recreational meeting at the manufacturing plant in Skokie. He thought the boss would be impressed.

A CONFESSION

It's time I got this off my chest. I'm 45 years old and some say I've accomplished a lot. I don't know what that means, but I do know my mom and dad think I'm a pretty wonderful guy.

Unfortunately, they don't have the facts. I had very little to do with my success. I don't feel badly about it. Everywhere I went I had a support group. In most instances whomever I worked with knew as much or more about the specifics of the issue as I did. It seemed foolish not to bow to their expertise. Whenever I did, I succeeded.

One day twenty years ago, I got up from my desk to stretch my legs. Before I knew it, I found myself in the heart of the organization. I thought I'd do a little bonding. "How's everyone," I inquired. I had no idea that simple question would open a flood of responses that would wash me into the parking lot. When I picked myself up, I realized they had a number of things on their mind.

Their concerns were real, perceptions accurate, and

frustrations high. It quickly occurred to me, if they could be that productive even though they were hampered, what could they do if I removed impediments to progress. I might conquer the world.

All of the sudden, I had a purpose. I would become the organizational bodyguard. Anything that hindered their ability to perform would be my lawful prey. I had always been combative (an emotional shortcoming) and now I could justify my behavior. I would patrol the perimeter (they now call it walk around management), and do battle. If something caused a disturbance, it got a bullet between the eyes. Only one month into the program and things were humming. In the absence of distractions, people were performing at an exceptional level.

I did have a problem. By 10 A.M. I'd fought sixteen skirmishes and wondered if I'd have anything left for the war. I needed a new approach. I decided to focus my energy exclusively in areas that impacted health. When I established that criterion, I knew my future battles would take place on environmental ground.

John Muir knows what I'm talking about. Surroundings determine the quality of existence. If I could create an environment that flourished, it seemed logical people would want to spend time in it. Taking the day off meant you would miss a lot of fun. Not doing your job could result in your being asked to leave the party.

The concept is so simple to understand, it's disturbing to observe how many people don't get it. To this day I walk into companies that haven't painted their walls in twenty years. The drinking fountain is broken, the carpet frayed, and the furniture looks like it functioned as barrier material in the Boxer Rebellion.

Forget that any human-factors engineer would tell you, performance improves as the physical environment gets better. What is more significant is the perception that's created. It can be expressed in groups of three. I don't care, you don't matter, I am lazy. If you, as their leader, don't act on issues of welfare, what other conclusion can be drawn? Possibly, the organization isn't worth it.

If that's the case, then your exuberance in asking them to give their all sounds hypocritical. I find most people despise hypocrisy. It is an insidious, deceitful personality disorder that eats away the fabric of trust, so necessary in building relationships.

Hypocrisy takes the stage in hundreds of different ways, but many of them are harmless. Who cares if the boss eats in his own private dining room, flies first class, and has a gold-plated pencil sharpener? His actions have no affect on you. If he's done his job, he's earned the perks.

On the other hand, there are people who are continually manipulating the system in order to prosper. Their self-absorbed indulgence, in furthering their own interests, does not allow for resources to be devoted to anyone else. Training programs are nonexistent because funds are needed for the executive washroom. A year-end bonus is more important than meeting a staffing level. A country club membership takes precedent over a Christmas party.

Believe it or not, people will even forgive and forget these sins, but if you are thinking you can operate with impunity anywhere you choose, I'm here to suggest, you think again. My experience has taught me there are three areas of concern that individuals, overtly or covertly will give no quarter. They may not physically attack you, but when you violate the sanctity of these environments, you have put their allegiance in jeopardy.

Each, in its own way is vital to health and accomplishment. If your leadership program does not allow for **Openness**, **Development** and **Fairness**, your judgment day is close at hand.

I'LL TAKE
THEM ALL

*What wisdom can you find
that is greater than kindness.*
— *Robert Coppola*

If accomplishment is a product of energy, than it doesn't take a Cal Tech graduate to understand the more energy you have at your fingertips, the better off you are. I realize many people don't see it that way. For a number of reasons: insecurity, bigotry, sexism and assorted other humanistic shortcomings, they want to limit who gets on the team.

Gates are closed, barriers are built and the organization becomes a one-dimensional representation of its leader's mind-set. I just don't understand it. I guess that's because I learned a long time ago, I'm not smart enough to know what another human being is capable of doing, until I've given them a chance.

OPENNESS

- Unobstructed entrance and exit.

- Accessible to all.

- Clear, frank, candid.

- Ready to transact business.

Take a look at Mikhail Gorbachev. The experts said he had the makings of a bureaucratic bumpkin, but when he got to sit in the driver's seat, he changed the world. Opportunity is a time proven way of generating ignition!

COURT-MARTIAL TO COMMAND SERGEANT MAJOR

Three weeks after assuming command of A Company, I had my first initiation into the Army's Uniform Code of Military Justice. The stage was set and it could have gone very similarly to the court-martial of Billy Budd. The villain carried the name William Peyton. He had been a problem child in the company for as long as he had been there, and had received numerous disciplinary actions. His recent forty-eight hour AWOL (Away Without Leave) had been a serious violation of division regulation, and now the discipline took on much greater significance. The company first sergeant had given me the paperwork and it was my responsibility to administer the punishment. He would be reduced in rank to the lowest level, have 75 percent of his pay taken away for four months and be given 90 days additional duty.

I sat behind my desk and asked to have Peyton brought in. He stood at attention in front of me and I inquired if he had anything to say. "Sir, this is bullshit," he replied. He then proceeded to verbally attack the procedure on ten different fronts. Racism, injustice, incompetence and a variety of other complaints came out of his mouth, with a passion and conviction that grabbed my attention.

During my brief tenure as company commander I had noticed Peyton was always the center of attention when he was in the area. It appeared he had the respect of the other young blacks in the company and exhibited leadership ability. In addition, even though I didn't state it, I agreed with his analysis of his section sergeant. He was at best marginal, and probably a racist. I took it all into account and given the emotion of the moment made a unilateral decision that I hoped would salvage him.

I ripped up the paperwork. His expression was one of astonishment, while the look on my top sergeant's face reflected tremendous anger. I wasn't finished. "Peyton, this company is a piece of shit and what I don't need around here are troublemakers. It appears from what I've seen, you have an ability to lead, and now I'm going to find out if your mouth has overloaded your ass (I always try to speak in a listener's vernacular). I'm going to make you an "Acting Sergeant" and transfer you from the clothing issue facility to the motor pool. I expect you to straighten it out. If you don't perform and decide you'd rather be a screwup, I will court-martial you next week."

When I made the decision not to punish Peyton, I violated a leadership principle. My action contradicted what my First Sergeant supported. In a way, it undermined his authority and I could understand his anger. My rationalization centered on the fact that the company was a mess and I had the responsibility to bring in a new way of doing things. As I explained it to him, crippling people is no way to get them to accomplish anything.

Yes, maybe Peyton was full of it, but if he is accurate in is assessment, let's err on the side of humanism. There is nothing we've done today that can't be reversed tomorrow. I've found when you give someone something they desire, they, more often than not, will work hard to keep it.

As it turned out, my minor gamble paid off. I also knew my action would be communicated through the company instantly. I hoped the message would be, the new guy operated differently than his predecessor.

I don't know if my action was the first break Peyton had received in his life, but he made the most of it. He turned out to be the best soldier in the company. Two decades later I ran into someone who had been with me in Korea and had made the army a career. As we discussed old times, Peyton's name came up. "Do you remember Peyton?" he asked. "Sure," I said. "Well, he's now a command sergeant major." It didn't surprise me.

Footnote: An "Acting Sergeant" has the authority and wears the stripes of a sergeant, but it is not an official rank. It is an expeditious way of getting a person in a leadership role. Command Sergeant Major is the highest enlisted rank in the Army.

For a number of years I thought about Peyton and my decision to give him a break. Every time I did, I patted myself on the back. Twenty-one years later, reality has humbled me. My actions with Peyton were nothing more than Leadership 101. The company needed energy, Peyton had some, so I used it.

It's simple physics. Using existing energy requires less energy than finding a new source of energy. Do you have any idea how much time, money and effort is squandered in organizations that have a high rate of personnel turnover. I've always used that as a barometer of how well an organization is led. When a leader is doing the right things people will kill to stay around. There is also another factor present when a leader hesitates to remove someone. The act itself says "I have failed." It's an indictment that any leader finds difficult to accept.

My actions were actually self-serving. I knew I only had so much energy to devote to this turnaround. Opening the door didn't require much; a simple turn of the knob. Well, that's not exactly correct. In reality, just letting people in means very little. If the initial act isn't followed with programs that allow Access, Inclusion and Participation, then you are probably better off trying to keep them out.

People are pretty smart. I've found they are very aware of what they are capable of contributing. When they are denied the opportunity to realize their potential they become highly dissatisfied. You'll recognize the symptoms: absenteeism, picket lines, disability claims, customer complaints and a host of other organizational ills. They are sending you a message and it doesn't require a cryptograph to decipher it. In Vietnam, dissatisfaction resulted in a practice called "fragging." When the troops weren't treated "according to Hoyle," a bullet in the back of the head or a hand grenade under a cot made the statement, "We're not happy."

It's incredible to see the lengths that some individuals go to turn their environment into a maximum security prison. It's incomprehensible because I can't remember the last significant contribution that came out of Siberia, Libya or San Quentin. Accomplishment results when freedom of movement, exchange of ideas and ability to think and act autonomously is encouraged. Obviously, leaders who create openness are considerably different than those that don't. They're less hypocritical; they treat others the way they want to be treated. They're more confident; they aren't afraid of mistakes. They're more talented; they've trained their subordinates to be responsive. They're smarter; they recognize everyone, in their own way, is capable of making a contribution.

Wardens think differently, but I can tell you from experience, it's not because of leadership ability. Quite the contrary. Their abusive behavior is the result of emotional deficiencies and laziness. Implementing a multifaceted employee-development program requires more ability and hard work than cracking the whip. Tyrants work twelve hours a day. Leaders are always on call.

HOW DO YOU SPELL TOUGH?

Based upon what I read about six executives high-lighted in a recent business periodical, I would spell it D-U-M-B. In this exposé, a number of leaders were described as "making your top dog look like a pussy-cat." The adjectives were very descriptive"punishing, intimidating, inhuman, explosive, bullying and heart-less." You had to feel sympathy for the employees that worked under them. Their suffocating dictatorial style got peoples' attention, but at what expense?

Is there a tangential association between how you are treated and what you become? You tell me. Give me the name of the last great leader who trained under Idi Amin, Fidel Castro or Joseph Stalin? What about the environment Don J. created. It looked like Cook County Jail. The question is, who is the criminal, Don or the inmates?

That's right, criminal! Have you ever looked up what constitutes a felony in the United States Penal Code? In many cases it's far less damaging than sup-pressing an individual's potential and stealing away their opportunity! Isn't verbal castigation more dam-aging than a fist in the face? One puts people out of commission for a couple days, while the other turns them into emotional eunuchs, crippling them for life.

I WOULDN'T IF I WERE YOU

Eight years after the conversation, I remember it as if it happened yesterday. I'd just finished working out and the phone rang. The caller identified himself as Marty Lewis and asked if he could have a few minutes to speak with me. I told him I wished my time was so valuable I didn't have any to give, but he could take all he needed.

He inquired if I still lifted weights. I said yes, and then prepared myself for an exercise equipment pitch. As he talked about physical fitness my brain started to make the connection. I interrupted him somewhere between analyzing squats and bench-pressing, and posed the question, "Are you Marty Lewis, as in Martin R. Lewis, the entrepreneur?" He acknowledged, one and the same, and then quickly got back to asking me how much I could curl. For the next hour the conversation focused exclusively on me, my interests and my family. Finally he got around to why he called.

He had heard my name and thought I might be looking for a new challenge. I told him I liked my job, worked for one of the best guys in the country, and didn't need a change. He accepted my response, thanked me for my time, and concluded the conversation.

As I hung up I thought, "different approach." The following Monday I mentioned the discussion to someone who had spent a number of years on Wall Street and knew the players. Lewis had a cult following. His reputation was that of a demanding, performance driven executive whose unique management style had made his company one of the most respected business entities in American industry. When Michael Milken made the decision to do his first public LBO, his choice for the experiment was Williamhouse-Regency Inc., Marty's company.

A week later Marty extended an invitation to lunch and I accepted. As I entered his office I thought I had gone into a curiosity shop. The walls were covered with memorabilia. Not the ego-reinforcing stuff that most chairmen display, but rather simple expressions of thanks and consideration from many of the company's employees.

I did notice an article from a Pittsburgh paper that chronicled his efforts to bring minority opportunity to the area thirty years earlier. He had risked everything but prevailed. Obviously, he understood there were more important things than a bank account.

To make a long story shorter, I couldn't help but be impressed by his humanism and decided to become part of his team. When I made the change I wondered whether it had been the right decision. It didn't take long to realize my instincts were correct.

Marty and I were traveling before a long holiday weekend and discussed what each of us had planned for the occasion. He informed me that he and his wife would be joining a number of old friends for a celebration. They hadn't seen each other in years and he enthusiastically awaited the reunion.

In between changing planes he called the office. Within seconds I could tell something was wrong. His face turned beet red and anger surfaced that bordered on rage. He hung up and told me he would not be returning to New York. He had just found out that sexual harassment allegations had been made against a senior manager and he would fly to the facility to address the issue.

All of a sudden, nothing else mattered. A trust had been violated and he had an obligation to be involved. His commitment to his employees superseded everything else. His conscience and sense of integrity compelled him to act; not at some convenient future date, but at that very moment.

I've had lots of battles with Marty over the years, but never when it comes to issues relating to the welfare of others. Whether he is lending money to an employee to buy a house, pay for college tuition or take care of a medical bill, Marty's never-ending sponsorship of his people tells them, their relationship is a two-way street.

Does Marty Lewis know how to spell tough? Abuse someone who works for him and find out for yourself.

THANK YOU, BOY SCOUTS

Over the years, I've had a few brushes with death and the fact I'm still here is more a result of luck than anything I did, with one exception. Eighteen years ago, on a trip across the country, I found myself in the great Rocky Mountains. I looked at my map and determined I had two hours worth of energy left. I bypassed Georgetown, Colorado, and an hour later found myself at Loveland Pass. At an elevation of 13,200 feet, it's a magnificent spot. I had just exited the tunnel and decided to stretch my legs. As I stepped out of my car, the cold night air activated my senses. The fact the temperature hovered around zero degrees didn't bother me. I looked up and a zillion stars gave a twinkling brilliance to the night sky. I decided I would sleep outdoors.

I saw a road ahead and drove up it until I found the perfect spot. I parked, pulled out my sleeping bag and climbed in. I spent about thirty minutes stargazing, and then fell asleep. As you know, dreams have a funny way of mirroring what is actually happening to your body. My dreams that night were about freezing to death in the artic.

I'm not sure what time I initially awakened but when I did, I knew something was wrong. My hands and feet were freezing. They had never been cold in a sleeping bag before. I reasoned it had something to do with the fact the still night air was now gusting at 30 mph. The wind-chill factor had turned zero degrees into minus twenty.

I looked up and the stars were gone. It's time to get going, I decided. I quickly packed up and jumped into my car. I hit the accelerator and ignition and a sickening clicking sound reported things weren't right. How could my battery be dead, my headlights were on? It didn't take long to realize the seriousness of what I was facing.

I knew all about how people die from exposure. Here I sat on a mountaintop, my body temperature dropping, a weather front moving in and a car that, for some unknown reason, wouldn't run. I had to get control of myself. I tried to start it again. Nothing. I needed time to figure it out, but the numbness in my body told me I'd better hurry up. Thank God, early morning light illuminated my surroundings. The area had been logged at some earlier date and wooden debris lay everywhere. Those cold damp logs were my salvation. I would turn a dormant energy source into a life-sustaining fire.

Had I not been a Boy Scout it wouldn't have happened. You see in the Boy Scouts, you learn starting fires is a function of scope and patience. The object is to start small and build on your success. To get ignition with damp wood requires you begin with almost microscopic tinder. When it ignites, you add slivers. As they catch fire, you jump to twigs, to sticks, to branches and finally logs. Leave out a step and your fire becomes a smoking cauldron.

I gathered what I thought I needed, shielded the fire on the leeward side of my car, and started the procedure. The perspiration on my brow was a harbinger that panic knocked at my door. Stick to the procedure, I kept telling myself. Don't circumvent the little guys. Imperceptibly the glow of the fire increased as every piece of wood fulfilled its responsibility. Without the tinder, the log would have never gotten to perform.

As my body temperature rose and I took charge of my senses, I addressed the automotive situation. When an engine doesn't start it's normally for one of two reasons: electrical or fuel. Electrically it appeared to be working, so I reasoned I had a fuel problem. Between the temperature and the reduced oxygen at that elevation, the fuel needed for ignition had changed dramatically. The solution, I hoped, rested in letting the excess liquid evaporate to a point where only the slightest vapors remained. I had my fingers crossed. Thirty minutes later as I drove down the mountain, I realized I had just been given another important lesson about combustion.

For me, that experience reinforced what is now a principle component in my leadership philosophy. It is impossible to determine contribution, until an opportunity to perform has been provided. Without that seemingly worthless timber, left by those loggers, I might not be here today. I'm not the only one who understands the concept.

PROCESS CONTROL AT ITS BEST

No, I'm not talking about General Electric. These activities occur in Marshalltown, Iowa. If you've never had the opportunity to do business with Mid-Iowa Workshops, find a reason. Jim DeLeve and the crew at this state-supported operation will go into my Hall of Fame.

In making the cut I've given them no concessions. They are, in an absolute sense, the most responsive organization I have ever encountered. What some uninitiated observer might find interesting is that their ability to perform is in no way impacted by the fact that the majority of their employees are physically and psychologically challenged.

Jim and his staff just find a way to maximize each individual's contribution. Whether it's assembling parts for Lenox Industries, sewing gun tube covers in support of Desert Storm or handling an outsourced project for Fisher Controls, the employees of MIW are incredible in their ability to get it right, each and every time they take on a job.

The monotony of their day-in, day-out activities would discourage the most responsible worker, but for them the boring repetition is energizing. Through Osoli, they have been given projects that cumulatively involved over a million separate steps, and I have yet to hear about a mistake. What does that tell me? Everyone has a place. If you don't think so, and want to get rid of a few one horsepower people, call Jim DeLeve. He'll take all he can get.

<u>N</u><u>OTES</u>

AN INALIENABLE RIGHT

When it rains you get wet, whether
you understand water or not.
— Bruce Killen

If you believe leadership involves helping others accomplish their goals, than I'm sure you recognize that it is more likely if they possess some kind of skill. Contribution normally comes with capability. Opening an environment is a prerequisite to getting your human resources in place, but if people don't have the ability to perform, their energy remains in abeyance. Successful organizations develop their people!

DEVELOPMENT

- To bring, grow or evolve to a more complete, complex or desirable state.

- To expand, to make more usable.

I've found as people are developed they can't wait to take on greater responsibility. When you look at the list of developmental opportunities at Microsoft Inc. it appears they are an accredited university. It's not altruism. Their leaders just understand the cost associated with having dysfunctional people is too great to accept. They recognize even major expenditures will generate tenfold returns. As undeniable as the concept of developing your people is to performance, there are still those that won't.

THE KING OF SILVER BULLETS

I had just taken over as national sales manager at International Paper Company, and consulted with my predecessor about the regional sales managers that would be working with me. When I asked him about one of them (we'll call him Spike), he delivered an enthusiastic response. Great guy! When you visit his region he'll have you out to his house for a barbecue. He makes the best martini in the world.

He didn't know that my criteria for evaluating a leader's performance has nothing to do with how much vermouth he puts in my drink. I'm not as interested in how he relates to me, as I am in the concern he shows toward his subordinates. In Spike's case, the results were abysmal.

His region exhibited the slowest growth in the country. His employees had the lowest average salary in the corporation, and no one could remember the last time they'd received supplementary training. Worst of all, even though they had the highest age and experience, not one had ever been tapped by the company for a position of greater responsibility.

When I met his team at our annual budget meeting, I thought I had entered a time warp. Here sat the Rip Van Winkles. They'd been on hold for two decades. I'd ask them a question and Spike would respond. My anger could hardly be controlled. After an hour I adjourned the meeting and told Spike I wanted to talk to him in private.

Upon entering his office, an ashen face indicated he knew he was at risk. He handed me his business plan for the coming year and it buckled my knees. He boasted his people had worked on it for a couple of weeks. I suspect they started putting it together the day after the previous year's had been accepted. I couldn't imagine how many man-hours had been wasted on its creation, but then I knew Spike understood smoke and mirrors.

I experienced a great deal of internal dissension. My aggressive side wanted to terminate him, but the leader in me recognized he happened to be a victim also. Why hadn't someone led him years earlier? Now, he belonged to me. "Spike, I don't care about your budget," I said. "You have one objective this year. You will develop your people." I briefly explained how I envisioned it would happen, and then left for the airport.

In Spike's case, he had crossed his Rubicon. He would be functional at best, but only with massive supervision and direction. On behalf of his employees we orchestrated promotions, salary increases and enrollment in company programs. They responded, and the region enjoyed more success than they had in a decade. He is now retired and I'll bet when someone asks him, "How good were you?" he'll reply, "The best!" I'm just not sure whether he means at paperwork, barbecue or silver bullets.

I never asked Spike why he kept his people barefoot and undeveloped. I suspect it had to do with insecurity. There are many who believe when you diminish others, in comparison, you look that much better.

John Stuart, CEO of ALCO Standard, has a different approach. The second he puts on his leader's cloak he can't wait to get his team up to speed. He understands the only measurement that means anything centers on collective effort. The group's achievement is his success.

If you don't have John's expertise, you probably have some questions as to where to begin. Start with an examination of the organizational MAPP. It will help you determine whether energy is active or passive. What standards are presently in place? Are objectives being met? Who's falling down on the job? Do people have the proper attitude? What is their level of skill? Skill is a product of manual dexterity, whereas attitude is a result of a mental orientation. Dan O'Brien had the skill, but his brain inhibited his ability to accomplish the goal.

His example is fairly common. In every environment there are people who aren't mentally with the program. My job is to get them psychologically adjusted. It's for that reason, whenever I take on a new challenge, I don't tiptoe into the environment. I want everyone to know I'm there, and because of it, they will get an opportunity to improve.

Immediately, I try to build expectation. I do it for two reasons. It puts pressure on me to make good on my promises, and it also creates optimism. When people think they are going to get smarter, stronger, and faster, they get excited. Excitement is a catalyst for combustion.

There's no magic in it. Everything centers around making people capable. Capability is the mechanical part of the equation. When you can analyze a balance sheet, assemble a computer, fill out an invoice or operate an eighteen wheeler, you have ability.

Physical development starts with education and training. I'm not talking about on-the-job instruction. It's effective, but only as a supplement to formal educational procedures. Put people in a classroom, give them an instructor, test their knowledge, and when they have completed the program, award them a diploma they are proud to hang on the wall.

Official instruction is needed for skill acquisition. Will it take time, money, effort and patience? Yes! Does it send the message, your people are worth the expense? Yes! Doesn't it also allow you to move the hurdle to a higher level.

I've found, as people develop ability, they want to use it. They take what you determined was an acceptable MAPP, and make a unilateral decision to raise it. You thought they were operating at 50 percent but they knew they were at 40. They can give you another 20 and not break sweat. Now multiply that by the number of people on your payroll.

Phil Knight, CEO of Nike, understands the concept perfectly. I suspect that's how he turned his company into the powerhouse it is today. He knows if he gets a ten percent improvement out of his nine thousand employees, he's picked up ninety thousand points. I'll bet he also recognizes the knife cuts both ways.

PENNY-WISE AND POUND FOOLISH

Ron Michelson had been a fraternity brother of mine at the University of Florida. When I bought a cabin at Lake Tahoe in 1977, he saw my down payment as his opportunity to become the next Franz Klammer.

The first call I received after closing came from Ron. "Let's go skiing," he said. I agreed to take a week off and accompany him to the slopes. As we drove to the mountain, I asked if he had skied before and he responded he hadn't. I suggested a lesson would be appropriate. He rejected the idea when he found out the cost. He said he would teach himself.

Because he never learned the fundamentals up front, each ski vacation became a nightmare. While his companions schussed down the mountain, Ron could be seen in the distance practicing his turns on the bunny slope. In the course of four years of watching him ski the Sierras, I saw him dislocate a shoulder, sprain a knee, break a finger and embarrass a date. On the upside, he could snowplow as well as any thirty-one-year old in the world.

The fifth year Ron didn't come west. I received his

call from Killington, Vermont. He enthusiastically told me he had hired their best instructor for the week, and had the time of his life. He just wanted me to know when he returned home, he would be changing his name to Jean Claude.

As foolish as the decision was to deprive himself of proper training, his actions were not abnormal. There is a tendency in all of us to shortcircuit the learning-curve. Who doesn't want to get to the heart of the issue? Never mind that your gas grill won't light, Johnny's bike only pedals backward and on the golf links, you are known as Lawrence of Arabia.

In matters such as these, self inflicted denial mandates no major penalty. In an organizational setting the same cannot be said. When Linda doesn't know how to properly work the switchboard, a lot of important calls are routed to the twilight zone. Had Gilbert been given leadership training, he wouldn't have terminated the employee-recognition program.

Look around you. Every time someone errs, ask yourself if it could have been avoided with proper training. If the answer is yes, get them back in school; not next month, but tomorrow. The sooner Harry understands the "K Factor," the more likely he will catch that $20,000 mistake. If you won't do it because it will save you money, do it because it will save your team.

What happens when someone is incapable of doing his or her job? More often than not, another person has to take up the slack. It's usually one of your more conscientious performers. If Jan has to carry Fred's water, she'll not only use up energy with the effort, but expend even more as she contemplates why.

The idea behind teamwork is that everyone carries a proportionate share of the load. I've never seen a championship organization that thought it would be okay to have some weak guys in the middle. The object is to create parity—not at the bottom, but at the top. When you neglect your weakest link, you weaken your strongest.

<u>N</u>OTES

KNOCKING AT YOUR DOOR

Our doubts are traitors, and
make us lose the good we oft
might win by fearing to attempt.
— William Shakespeare

Upon assuming a leadership role, wouldn't it be nice if the environment was contaminant free, the objective lay unobstructed, and your team's intent was as pure as the driven snow? If that were the case, I suspect the organization could get along without you. In most instances you'll find the place is polluted, the objective sits in a minefield, and your newly acquired team just spent the last few years working for a guy by the name of Rasputin.

Believe it or not, this scenario isn't all bad. I'm sure you remember leadership isn't about maintaining the status quo. The only purpose in giving you the job was to make things better. I think you can see the opportunity to apply your craft is needed more in an organization that is failing than one described as Shangri-la. It doesn't take great acumen to understand if you are good at leading, you will spend a lot of time in the muck and mire. I have, and I will tell you there is no better place to be.

I didn't always feel that way. There was a period in my life whenever I accepted a new challenge, I contemplated failing. I fear failure as much as the next person. It wasn't until my fourth or fifth leadership assignment that it finally came to me. When it did, I realized I couldn't fail. It has to do with the nature of teams, and the fact that they are always in transition. If the guy before you ruined the players, many of the nonperformers have left. They have been replaced by others who have a different psychological orientation.

Not everyone has grown up under bad leadership. Whether they arrived yesterday or four years ago, they've been waiting for you! They had no desire to operate at 50 percent, but the environment didn't give them an option. Thanks to circumstance, they can now get back in the race. These are your Thoroughbreds.

In addition, you'll find individuals who have not been contaminated, nor have they been energized. Somewhere in their upbringing they had exposure to leadership, and are aware of what can be accomplished with proper direction. They will be receptive to what you give. Meet the organizational Rookies.

Your challenge is the The Whipped Dogs (WD). You don't have to own a kennel to appreciate the label. If a dog received abuse in its formative years it may never shake the emotional scars. Even though you played no part in the mistreatment, you will suffer the burden of their insecurity ad infinitum.

Certainly, when I use the term, I'm speaking figuratively. People are not dogs and although there may be similarities in the behavior that follows abuse, unlike a canine, mental torment doesn't necessarily have to be a life sentence.

Remember what I said about hope? Doesn't it "spring eternal"? If so, then by virtue of their humanness, they hope that you are a horse they can ride. Now it's up to you to climb through that window of opportunity.

A REVELATION

I wish I could say I figured it out with my first leadership challenge, but if I did, I'd be lying. As a matter of fact, I don't think I totally understood it until a decade of "fits and starts." Early on, I thought all I had to do was give people ability. Once they had it, they would want to pick up a longer pole. At the time, I had no idea when I developed their skill, my job was only a third complete.

Much to my surprise, I soon found out, by merely making Henry able, it didn't necessarily make him willing. If there was injustice in that, it came with the fact that his reluctance to get going had nothing to do with me. Hank was a product of his past and because of it, he was afraid.

FEAR

- Shun; falter; cower; avoid; lose courage; be alarmed; scared; live in

terror; flinch; cringe; tremble;
dare not.

It didn't matter where the fear came from, it now belonged to me. The responsibility to rid him of it was mine. I knew, if he was going to climb the Spectrum of Accomplishment, "dare not" would have to be replaced by "dare a lot."

> *"Complacency is the hobgoblin of*
> *small minds and little men."*
> — *Carl Sandberg*

I didn't want him to think he had to stick his neck in a guillotine, but I thought he should know I expected a return on my investment. If it meant putting himself at risk, so be it.

I've found when individuals believe there is potential danger, they get energized. When someone is presented with a situation that has an upside and a downside, they wake up. The opportunity for gain is juxtaposed against the penalty for failure, and a decision is made to proceed. That is, unless fear contaminates the process.

I've found fear to be a debilitating, constrictive, enervating emotion. There is nothing in how the term is defined that would make anyone but a blockhead think fear generates energy. Just ask Lieutenant Colonel James T. Durgen (an alias).

PATTON OR PUTZ

If I live another hundred years, I doubt I will ever see his equal. If there is a hell, I pity Satan when

Durgen shows up. Gold ascot, cavalry spurs, armor beret, silver-plated pistol, tanker boots and swagger stick were just the tip of the psychological iceberg.

He lived to put people in fear. In watching him in action I couldn't fathom why anyone would search for conflict in every encounter. Obviously, it filled an emotional void. Durgen's arrogant, abusive, confrontational manner had emasculated his entire organization. No one made a move without Jimbo's blessing. His leadership persona consisted of four parts pompous ass, six parts control freak, with a smattering of quirks adopted from Ivan the Terrible. Call it luck, luck or luck, somehow he had survived his Neanderthal nature. All that was about to change.

In the summer of 1976, I'd been given the job of evaluating his unit during a four day, combined arms, tactical readiness test. His tank battalion had the mission of kicking off the land assault portion of the operation. The division commander had invited a number of Pentagon VIPs down to observe the firepower display. Without getting into a detailed explanation of how these things work, suffice it to say, everything hinges on a coordinated effort. Everyone has to be in their appointed place and ready to go, at a prescribed time.

The unit had spent a month rehearsing their part of the operation and could now perform it in their sleep. As it turned out, had they remained unconscious, they would have been better off.

During the "real deal," as they moved toward the line of departure, something unexpected happened. Durgen's radio went on the blink, and with it, his career aspirations. As he popped in and out of his tank's turret, he resembled a prairie dog in angst. I could see the panic on his face. He knew the battalion would not move without his orders, and he had no way to give them. He was right! Paralyzed by fear, eighty-eight tanks remained frozen in their tracks. When I heard the Commanding General profanely inquire as to the whereabouts of Durgen's Battalion, I got the feeling, justice was about to be served.

At the end of the exercise, I handed him his failing grade and headed out. As I drove down the interstate I felt energized. Not by virtue of helping a bad guy get what he deserved, but rather because another one of my leadership beliefs had just been reinforced: When someone creates an environment of fear, the knife cuts only one way!

As pathetic as people like this are, we won't waste time critiquing them. They're on a path to extinction. When a leader feels a need to pull intimidation out of its sheath, it normally results in self-mutilation. I haven't seen any bonafide, All-American tyrants in quite a while. They bled to death, imploded or went belly up, when their people left.

Unfortunately, that only eliminates the presence of one kind of fear. I think it's recognized, the genesis of most fear isn't the result of some external presence. If it were, when the Big Bad Wolf showed up at your birthday party, everyone would scream. In actuality, only some cower in the corner. There are those that aren't scared by Frankenstein, Vampira or Ted Smith. It comes with being physically and mentally in shape.

Fear on the other hand, is a psychological reaction to doubt. People who fear the most are usually developed the least. When you aren't prepared to wrestle the "Creature from Poughkeepsie" three out of four falls, the smartest thing to do is run away. I won't indict the Whipped Dogs for what comes naturally. They are a product of their upbringing. It's not abnormal when you recognize you are in over your head, to look for safety.

On the flip side, the Thoroughbreds eating cake on the couch, aren't worried. If Ted starts trouble, they will whip his ass. They probably won't have to, because most bullies don't mess with individuals who are fit. Here you have the same threat, but two different reactions. One is the result of fear, while the other is a manifestation of confidence.

I think that's how the idea of leaders being out in front came about. If the guy in charge shows the way, then it must be all right. You've heard the slogans: *Follow Me, Lead by Example, Dare to Be First, First by Far.* The fact is, leaders don't blaze trails to show it's safe, they do it because it is a functional way to get others on board.

Dwight Eisenhower understood the concept. He explained it to a young lieutenant before a major engagement. If you take an object and connect it to a length of rope and push from behind, the rope bends and the object remains stationary. On the other hand, if you get in front and pull, you will get substantial movement.

He's right of course, but his analogy has greater worth in theoretical terms than practical application. If you are leading a group and each member is no farther away than the toss of a boomerang, it's easy to run over and pull them through.

In today's environment, organizational evolution and technology has changed the landscape. Teams of men and women no longer have to work under the same umbrella. How are you going to handle the situation, when ten people in six different cities need your help. I'd suggest, not very well. There just isn't enough rope.

For leaders who operate at Mach 2, it never becomes an issue. They understand accomplishment has always been a product of internal combustion. Real success comes when individuals are capable of resolving their own problems.

"WORLD BEATER" OR TIN CUP

One of the most intellectually stimulating experiences of my life occurred serendipidously a few years ago, with help from a Lebanese industrialist. My invitation had come two days earlier, when I received a phone call from the director of personnel for Interstate Resources, an American subsidiary of INDEVCO (Industrial Development Corporation). The Chairman and founder would be coming to the U.S. and desired to meet with me in Washington. I wasn't up on my Middle Eastern "Who's Who," but I liked D.C., so I agreed to make the trip.

In the interim, I did a little research on the parent company and found out they were a diversified conglomerate with operations around the world. I couldn't fathom why Georges Frem wanted to talk to me.

As it turned out, he was in search of a president for one of his companies, but that has no relevance to this story. What is significant is what transpired during the time we were together.

Somewhere in the initial stages of our discussion the issue of leadership came up. Upon hearing the word, Georges' transformation from Arab sage to Baptist preacher occurred instantly. Apparently he had waited a long time to deliver his sermon.

He told me when he started INDEVCO his leadership style approximated that of any entrepreneur. Everything funneled through him. As the company prospered and grew, he found it increasingly difficult to manage the extremely diverse operational entities. At that point, he had a decision to make. Should he establish even tighter management controls and continue to call the shots, or take a diametrical approach?

He knew one course of action would ultimately lead to stagnation and failure, while the other would necessitate a change in a leadership style that had worked successfully for years.

He understood a wrong decision would have dire consequences. When he voted in favor of delegating responsibility he felt confident he had secured the organization's future success.

Following that decision, he instituted an unparalleled proactive employee-development program. He not only wanted people ready for what they would encounter in their job, he wanted them developed in every aspect of their human existence. He recognized the inextricable link between an individual's personal and professional life. His actions stated unequivocally, that he understood the whole was the sum of all its parts.

When the discussion concluded ten hours later, I suffered from mental exhaustion. But, I felt exuberance over the fact that every leadership principle I ever contemplated had just been reinforced by an acclaimed business leader.

A few weeks later, I relayed the experience to a friend. Understandably, he inquired as to the extent of our discussion. I started to paint a picture of two minds exploring the universe, and then realized if I did, it would be a distortion of what actually transpired. In reflecting back, even though we had spent a day together and touched on a multitude of topics, the conversation transcended nothing beyond preparation.

Recently a mutual acquaintance asked me if I knew what Georges was presently doing. I responded I didn't, but in actuality, I probably did. He is still introducing programs that guarantee the employees in his organization are prepared to succeed.

<u>N</u>OTES

ON YOUR MARK

*People seldom improve when
they have no other model but
themselves to copy.*
— *Oliver Goldsmith*

Success! Could there be any sweeter sounding word. I don't think so. It governs our entire existence. From the cradle to the grave, virtually everything someone does, in one way or another, has to do with the pursuit of success.

The first success of the day starts with your alarm going off and the final one comes when you enter slumber land. If you didn't think going to sleep meant achieving success, talk to an insomniac. Some people define success as having a positive outcome from some action. If that's the case, then every day individuals are successful in countless numbers of ways. I agree, but I'm not as concerned with the achievement aspect of success as I am with its impact on energy.

Do you remember the locker room of the 1993 Superbowl champions? How about those guys from Buffalo? Here, the Buffalo Bills had an extraordinary history of success, and yet, at that moment in time, their defeat had incapacitated them. I guess what they say about success is true. "It is in the eyes of the beholder."

Shout "Hallelujah," because it's for that reason your opportunities to use it as an energizing agent are endless. You can decide When, Where, Why and How. All you need to know is how to deal the card. Let's start the education by breaking down what some have described as an elusive subject into more earthly components.

When I think about success, I don't see it so much as a goal as I do a catalyst. I can't control how individuals are going to interpret their success, but I do have dominion over the program that enables it to happen. In my mind, the recipe for success involves three ingredients: preparation, application and feedback.

If people don't think they have a chance of winning, there is a real possibility they will never run the race. When someone is prepared, they can't wait to get in the blocks. In all my years of watching track and field events, I don't remember anyone saying "no" when the judge commanded, "Runners take your mark."

It's not as if there isn't risk involved. Standing in the warm-up area in their $600 running suits, they look like world champs. Mom and dad are proud, the fans sit in adulation and the camera crews are ready. One hundred and ten meters down the track they envision fame and fortune.

That is, unless they are a Whipped Dog. Their lack of preparation forces a different picture to materialize. They could get a bad start, trip on a hurdle or be out-run by anyone of nine competitors. They are well aware of the aftereffects of failure. At the very least, their sponsor will want their shoes back.

I've found the fear of failure is a stronger motivating force than the desire to succeed. If failing has such an enervating impact on a Thoroughbred, what do you think a legacy of it has done to the energy of a WD? Is it any wonder they have no desire to participate. They would rather exist in a state of "operational purgatory" (they do nothing that elevates their position, nor do their actions relegate them to eternal damnation) than risk failing. Enter the leader. Terry Kinnamon, president of Neenah Paper, understands getting people to believe they can succeed is the spark that will get ignition, but it does not a fire make.

The real energy comes when people actually experience success. That's where you come in. Your job as a leader is to create as much of it as possible. "Follow me and you will succeed" has always had greater appeal than "together we will die."

If you are wondering where to start, I would suggest anywhere you can. I didn't always feel that way. In my early leadership days, I saw success as an End Game. I think my view came about as a result of Santa bringing me a set of Lincoln Logs.

Upon opening them, I immediately constructed the roof. I was disappointed to learn I couldn't use it until I built a supporting structure. I went back and painstakingly, log by log, built the foundation. In mathematical terms, it's called a linear approach. When the instructions finally showed a picture of a roof, I knew I had achieved my goal.

As I grew older, I applied the same linear methods to leadership. I never thought about step six until five had been completed. I knew success would come with time. It would take a while, but the Pot of Gold was worth the wait.

The problem arose when I needed to expedite the process. With my newfound responsibility came a timetable for accomplishment, considerably shorter than Darwin's.

KOREA REVISITED

D-Day had arrived, March 10, 1973! Alpha Company, 2nd S&T would be under my command. I didn't sleep the night before, because I knew the foundation for what I'd try to accomplish would start with the morning formation. During the first thirty minutes of our relationship, the men of Alpha Company would start to form an opinion about me. Nobody needed to tell me first impressions were important.

Had I thought I'd be addressing a group of Thoroughbreds, I'd have been less anxious. But, I knew when you talk about the rewards of excellence to Whipped Dogs, you might as well be speaking Martian. Given their history of failure, our views on the subject would be planets apart. What could I possibly say that would trigger a reaction. I contemplated showing them how I could shoot an M-79 from the hip, but then realized these supply agents probably didn't care.

I looked over my menu of motivational offerings, and decided to go with speech 107: Climbing Out of the Abyss. It's pretty standard stuff. Here's where we are. Here's where we want to go. Here's what we have to do to get there. Here's what will happen when we're successful. Throw in a quote about a guy named Gipper, and you are on your way.

As I delivered it, the emotionless faces in front of me indicated my words fell on deaf ears. My strategy had been wrong. I had cast out self-respect as a lure and no one bit. After about twenty minutes, I figured I'd bring the nonevent to closure. Then I remembered I had forgotten to mention the upcoming physical fitness test. When I did, I immediately saw a reaction from a few individuals in the formation.

While the company had averaged an abysmal 315 (300 being the MAPP) on the prior test, there were a few Thoroughbreds who had done very well. I figured if I could get them to replicate their performance, I could recognize their success.

I started to encourage everyone to give their best and then realized my invitation would be wasted on the masses. This conversation would be between me, and anyone that had enough energy to respond. Years of playing organized athletics had given me a reference guide on how to get people excited. The guys who delivered the best halftime pep talks always had a lot of energy. It's physics again; energy creates energy.

I flipped the psychological switch and my lips revved up to the red line. I told them I was as bad a Mother as any on the block and they were about to witness, by means of the PT test, why Airborne Rangers were the physical studs of the universe. I went on for a couple minutes and decided I'd better shutdown when I almost told them I could climb the Matterhorn barefoot.

I had never scored less than five hundred (the maximum) on the event and decided to use that knowledge to my advantage. It would start with a challenge.

CHALLENGE

- To dare.

- To take part in a contest.

- Demanding task that requires dedication.

- A call to climb to a higher level.

I've found when you ask people to do more, if the request is reasonable, they will give it their best shot. There are those that believe challenging people puts them in fear. I've found just the opposite. Taking part in contests is what living is about. I don't think I've ever been to a picnic where someone didn't break out the volleyball net. Turn on the TV, pick up the paper or listen to the radio and a majority of what you see and hear is about challenges: athletic, business, political, academic or military.

Since our earliest years we have been challenged. What do you think that schoolyard game, breaking the chain, entailed. When the entreatment came to "come on over," did you skip to those awaiting arms? Hell no, you got going as fast as your little legs would carry you. When you made contact, your objective transcended busting a grip — you wanted to knock down the entire chain.

Challenging people is the foundation to our educational system. That's the purpose behind having twelve grades. It's academia's way of telling you, what will happen in eighth grade is more difficult than second. If you weren't supposed to be challenged, you would do first grade twelve times.

While Thoroughbreds and Rookies readily accept challenges, apathy and fear make Whipped Dogs reluctant. In this particular case I didn't care because I figured only a small percentage of the population would be listening. If I could get a few to take the bait, I could get things going.

My boasts were starting to generate a reaction. While the men may not have been proud of their organization, they took pride in their physical prowess. Even though many had barely scored above the minimum on the "run, dodge and jump," they could be seen dunking basketballs at the gym every weekend.

I decided to create a little antipathy (teams respond to a common enemy). "Men, last night at the officer's club, a commander in the 1/23 Infantry told me quartermaster troops are wimps (I lied). I have no way of knowing, because you guys are the first I've seen. I do know I'm going to whip your ass on next week's fitness test. If any one of you proves me wrong and beats my score, I'll give you a seven day pass." I dismissed the formation and returned to my office.

Shortly thereafter one of the company's lieutenants asked if he could talk to me. He had a legitimate concern. He knew their performance on the previous test had been a result of attitude, not ability. Now that a seven-day pass had entered the picture, he worried a number of these former high school athletes would take me on. What if they beat me. The company could ill afford to have people away. I told him not to worry. I'd always maxed the test so the best anyone could achieve would be a tie. He breathed a sigh of relief but then inquired, "What if you trip?"

DREAMS DO COME TRUE

The day of the exam I told the First Sergeant to call a midday formation so we could march to the testing area. As I watched the company fall in, I had a feeling something had changed, but I couldn't put my finger on it. For the first time since I'd taken command there were no stragglers. As they stood there "shuckin and jivin" I thought this can't be true; these guys actually look like they are alive.

Halfway over, one of the Thoroughbreds started a jody call (a military song usually about someone's mother or girlfriend that begs for a reply). Surprisingly, most of the company responded. Could it be true? Their voices sounded energetic. Then it came to me. Virtually everyone in that formation thought, at the end of the test, they would be receiving a seven-day pass. A nineteen-year-old could have a lot of fun in a week in Korea.

When we reached the obstacle course, they requested

I go first, but I knew when my 500 hit the scoreboard, the majority would be back at 315. In that they didn't know how high I would score, they would have to go all out. I would perform last.

I asked my First Sergeant to let me know the individual scores as soon as the men completed their events. I could feel energy being expended but had no way of knowing how much. When the results were brought to me, I couldn't believe my eyes. I didn't see one score below 470. The officers were crazed with joy. The men finished and I took the stage. The entire company walked me through the events: forty-yard low crawl-100; overhead bars-100; sit-ups-100; run, dodge and jump-100.

On the final event I thought about slowing up, to allow a number of men to beat me. It would have optimized my ability to reward their performance, but suboptimized a perception I needed to create of myself as their leader. I wanted them to think I was invincible. It's basic psychology. When the going is tough, people are more likely to follow Rambo than Pinky Lee. I decided to finish in a blaze of glory: two mile run-100, Total-500.

My guys were quick on the uptake. By the time I'd finished the third event, you could see their energy dissipating. They knew they'd been sandbagged. Fading rapidly were thoughts of breakfast at Miss Kim's Bakery and Dance Hall. What they didn't know is when I said they wouldn't beat me, I didn't say they couldn't win. The last time I looked, leaders controlled the playing field.

FIREFIGHTER OR PUBLIC SPEAKER

Believe it or not, a majority of people would rather fight a blaze then give a speech. Todd Richardson fell into that category. When I was the Manager of Sales and Marketing for the Western Region of International Paper, Todd arrived on my doorstep as a squeaky-clean, energetic employee and informed me he wanted to conquer the world. I thought the sooner I got him in action, the better.

I told him to set up a series of meetings, whereby he would introduce himself, give an information briefing on our company, and answer any questions that the audience had.

At the time, I didn't realize he had never given a speech. I thought I had set a reasonable MAPP; but in this case, his perception of the event approximated a swim across the English Channel with bowling balls tied to his feet.

I decided to participate in the first one to show support. As we set the room for a group of eighty-five, I noticed he was sweating profusely. The temperature on the thermostat read sixty-five, so I knew it had nothing to do with being overheated. The water dripping on the floor came from an anxiety attack. I recognized the symptoms and immediately asked if he had ever spoken in public. His cotton mouthed response indicated he hadn't.

Alert! Alert! Alert!

I'm not sure how someone else would have interpreted the situation, but I knew I had an energy crisis. I should have asked him at the time of establishing his MAPP if he thought he could do it.

As his leader, it now fell on me to extricate him. The difficulty lay not so much in saving him, as it did with doing it while preserving as much energy as possible. Using memory retrieval, I pulled up the Universal Energy Chart. As I reviewed it in my mind, I realized a potentially incapacitating event was about to begin. There were three ways major energy would be lost. Two impacted Todd; embarrassment and humiliation, while the third affected our relationship: betrayal. My lack of insight had put him in jeopardy.

On the combustion side of the ledger, I also had energy creating opportunities. Sensitivity, involvement and a decisive course of action, would send a message he was not alone.

I said "Todd, I've decided I need to talk to these guys about some changes in our product offering so I'll take the first fifty minutes. When I'm finished, I'll introduce you. Give them a brief background on yourself and we'll call it a day." The 360-degree smile on his face told me my instincts had been correct.

Now, I prayed he wouldn't forget his name. He didn't, and as he gained confidence in the sound of his voice, he spoke beyond what I'd instructed. I guess he realized, if he got in trouble, he had me as an escape hatch.

As we proceeded to give these presentations over a two-month period, the format never changed, with one exception. As he progressed, I would give him an ever-increasing portion of the program. One day, as we were setting up for our fifteenth encounter, he turned to me and confidently said, "I'll take this one on my own!"

A few years later I received a call from a friend who had witnessed his debut as a public speaker. She told me she'd just returned from a graphic arts conference, and although most of the speakers were terrible, one stood out. "Could I guess who?" she asked. "Todd Richardson," I said.

While I take satisfaction in knowing I helped someone succeed, I no longer attribute it to some special insight that I possess. Mike Anderson, a waiter/leader at Ralph and Kacoo's seafood grill in New Orleans understands the concept perfectly.

Not long ago, I was at R&K's eating dinner when a table of drunks next to me grabbed an apprentice waiter who was passsing by their table. They aggressively inquired as to what fish on the menu could be blackened. The apprentice stood blank-faced because he didn't know the answer. I could feel his embarrassment and wanted to assist him, when out of nowhere, Mike Anderson arrived on the scene. Like most leaders, he was happy to play the role of mother hen. He looked at the inquisitors and stated Leon was the restaurant's "gumbo man" and didn't have time for fish. He would be happy to answer their questions. You could see the appreciation on Leon's face, and as they walked away, Mike patted him on the shoulder and said "No big deal."

BACK TO THE TRACK

Even though the circumstances between Todd Richardson and the men of Alpha Company were different, my motive in both situations happened to be the same. I knew I could only reward effort if I could get someone to succeed.

Alpha Company's performance had exceeded my wildest expectations and now it fell upon me to keep the energy active. I gave them a "you guys are unbelievable" pitch and declared everyone would get a three-day pass. The two individuals who tied me, would receive the seven-day version.

The group roared its approval. I had to capitalize on what just happened. I told my officers I wanted people on leave immediately. Establishing credibility is critical in the incipient stages of a relationship.

The next afternoon, the word came down from headquarters that Alpha Company had placed first among all divisional units. Nobody could believe, in an infantry division, quartermaster troops took the blue ribbon. A giant killer had just been born.

I requested the battalion commander write a congratulatory letter (an enhancer). I called "Wonder Boy," a Lieutenant who served as a deejay on the division's radio network, and asked if he would announce the results (an energizer). In that he was an infantryman he stated he had no desire to embarrass his comrades. That was, until I offered him a case of steaks. Greed plus an understanding of what made for good entertainment, delivered a gift from heaven. We timed his broadcast with the morning formation and had the loudspeakers turned up high.

His reading of the division news started mildly enough and then the showman in him took control. Castigating the infantry units for allowing a quarter-master company to "stomp their ass," his ranting and raving could be heard in Pyongyang. He suggested a role reversal would be appropriate. Let the men of Alpha Company fight and the fighting men dispense milk. He went on for a few minutes and with each comment I looked into the eyes of my men and could see they were turning into atomic reactors.

While I took pride in their achievement, something far more significant grabbed my attention. Standing in front of me stood a group of men with a level of energy I hadn't expected to see for months. Somehow, through a combination of luck (I could have assumed command a week after the Physical Fitness Test) and a little trickery, the time it took to accomplish something had been dramatically compressed. By accident, the company had jumped from step one to ten.

These individuals had not been prepared to succeed, and yet they pulled out a Victory. It appeared I'd been all wrong. Success didn't have to be an End Game; it could be an "anywhere" game. Why couldn't I create success at the beginning. I realized I could. If success engenders energy, it seemed logical, the sooner I could get it, the better off I'd be.

In the following months the company won the division blood drive, softball championship and flag football championship, scored the highest on the Tactical Readiness Test and Annual General Inspection. Somewhere in the middle of all this, the division commander was so proud of his supply organization, he invited me to brief the Chairman of the Joint Chiefs about our operation. By the time I relinquished command, Alpha Company ranked number one in the division. Once again people had pulled me through. I'm not being modest when I say I had nothing to do with the company's success, because I didn't. I will take credit for having a big mouth.

LEADERSHIP MATH

Even though I believe intuition is a valuable leadership attribute, there are situations when it helps to be a rocket scientist. I found out how brainpower could supplement brawn in a graduate school course I took titled Deterministic Modeling.

While the name sounded impressive, the class was nothing more than fifteen weeks of finding empirical solutions to problems. Most of it had no applicability until we came to the section on probability and statistics.

Surprisingly, I started to learn something about causal relationships. Before the education, I thought I could easily identify what effect one action had on another. As time went on, I realized it was impossible, until I worked through a series of mathematical formulas. In trying to assess the relationship of three factors in a seemingly simple word problem, you could get into four pages of calculations. Upon completion, you found out two of the events that appeared to have no relationship were, in fact, inextricably entwined.

I won't pursue this much further because, as we know, when we're dealing with the human brain, the arena is highly nondeterministic. I do think it's important though, that you at least understand the concept of exclusivity.

For our purpose, let's focus on the term "mutually exclusive." Simply stated, when two events are mutually exclusive, they don't share anything in common. For example, deceit is exclusive from integrity. I bring this to your attention because there are individuals who believe you can isolate behavior. Castigating an employee in public on Monday will have no impact on gaining a commitment from him or her on Friday. Disrespect is in no way connected to loyalty. For your information, in the game of leading, nothing is mutually exclusive. Every action, in one way or another, has an impact on the whole.

If good leadership generates a five BTU gain on Tuesday and bad leadership losses you seven BTU's on Wednesday, you net out a minus two going into Thursday. Five steps forward and seven steps back is no way to get people to a higher MAPP.

It doesn't take much to figure out you always want to play the energy hand. Take a look at the Universal Energy Chart and you can quickly identify what cards to leave in the deck. If you are going to generate results at supersonic speeds, it should be obvious the quicker you locate the heat, the sooner the results will come. In my experience, I've found energy exists predominantly in three areas, in descending order of magnitude: **Self Image, Material Gain, Crime and Punishment.**

I always start by trying to get people excited through ego impacting activities: Inclusion, Recognition, Trust, Pride, Integrity, Loyalty or Teamwork. If it isn't working, I'm quick to play another card.

When I stood in front of the formation and tried to hook them on Contribution, I got nowhere. When Pride and Reward entered the picture, I started to get some action. The logic behind the approach is pretty sound. We oftentimes don't know what hand someone is holding. We never know for sure what card is playable. A three, four, five, six or eight is a loser, but a seven takes the pot.

If a Whipped Dog has been numbed through abuse, your threat of kicking them in the head probably won't get much reaction. An individual who has prospered under leadership may not get as excited about a Reward as one who hasn't. The object is to play the right card at the appropriate time. Frequently, it is no more difficult than starting the game with a question.

When I issue a challenge, I know it can be misinterpreted. What a Thoroughbred sees as a compliment, (I think you are better than your MAPP), a WD may view as a threat (I'm out to get you). It's for that reason I don't challenge people with unilateral proclamations.

I always ask Leroy what he thinks about taking on a greater challenge. Does he mind if I raise the bar? I'm never sure what the answer will be. Confidence waxes and wanes with circumstance. His knowledge of land navigation will get him down the Appalachian trail but when he hears his next trip is the Amazon, he may have doubts. Fear depletes energy.

I'm interested in getting Leroy over the bar, not catching it in his teeth. My responsibility is to ensure every challenge results in success.

A BIRD, A PLANE OR A BULLET

The organization that had responsibility for seeing approximately $2 billion worth of fine printing paper made it to the market had a history of marginal performance in the area of service.

A select group of key executives (an advisory council) from International Paper Company's customer base would meet annually and critique the marketing issues of the day. While their attitude ebbed and flowed in discussing most topics, their opinion about customer service never changed. At the conclusion of each meeting they would give an evaluation of the company. In the area of service, IP ranked, in their view, as having the worst in the industry.

After a number of years of this kind of input, the Group Executive who ran the business determined he'd had enough. On the way to the airport, he stated, effective immediately, the customer service operation would report to me. I already had enough responsibility and this new development would double it. Had I not understood energy, I probably would have gotten my résumé in order. I did, though, so I said great!

I knew I couldn't do it by myself, so I asked for one of the most talented young leaders in the company, Ray Rabbitt, to function as my implementor.

Together we did an energy analysis. What programs were in place to create energy? None! What in the environment depleted energy? Much!

We interviewed everyone in the customer-service organization individually and determined people had no career path, they were underpaid, underrecognized, underrewarded, and virtually unaccountable. In addition, the company's Management Information capability was behind the times. Also, even though customer service occupied a critical position in the marketing effort, the group had been ignored and isolated from the decision-making process.

I assembled the group and told them I felt we had identified various problem areas and I would deliver my plan of action within a week.

In a bureaucratic monster like International Paper, nothing moves in seven days, but because this problem had received such visibility, my requests were given priority.

MY STRATEGY

Attack every problem immediately through energy creating programs.

Step 1 *Establish four customer-service position levels: Trainee, Customer Service Representative, Senior Representative, Supervisor.*

Prior to this change, whether you were an incompetent, on the job six months, or a Thoroughbred with twenty years service, you carried the same title— Customer Service Representative. It didn't take much to figure out that was no way to motivate people. Succeed or fail, and you remained the same.

The new structure institutionalized our ability to recognize performance. It also allowed for an individual to have a career path. At school, when Johnny was asked, "What's your daddy's title?" he no longer had to reply, "No change." Now that we had the structure, we could immediately promote 25 percent of the group and adjust salaries accordingly. The fire had been started.

Step 2 *Put through a major capital expenditure to upgrade the computer system.*

Even though it would takes months to get it on line, the expectation that they would be able to perform at a higher level got people excited.

Step 3 *Institute a product-line interface program.*

I mandated once a week, before business hours, product line managers would update the customer service department on their activities. As a way of thanking the group for showing up, the managers had to bring breakfast. I knew the competitive spirit between managers would kick in and it wouldn't be long before gravlax and lingonberry torts replaced donuts.

Even though participation was voluntary, the product managers always played to a packed house. Whether it had to do with people wanting a free breakfast (a reward), or were excited to be included in the marketing effort (an ego stroke) didn't matter. The objective of the session centered on getting the team communicating. Who cares what card made it happen?

Step 4 *Implement the Golden Bullet Program.*

I chose a bullet for the icon because, as I told them, we were at economic war. To win, you needed ammunition. When I introduced the program, I knew it would ignite controversy. I didn't care. My objective centered on raising the MAPP, and I could think of no better way of doing it than by getting everyone involved. In order for that to occur, I reasoned I would have to tap three energy sources: Ego, Gain and Accountability.

The program centered around what I called a Bulletgram: a self-addressed, postage-paid, return-postcard that, when received, would be a catalyst for action.

A packet of grams, along with accompanying correspondence, would be sent to all our customers. My letter stated we were making dramatic changes to improve our service and I needed their help. If they,

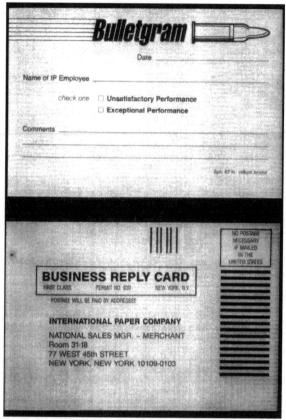

by means of a Bulletgram, would let me know which CSR's were doing an outstanding job, as well as those which were deficient, I would take appropriate action.

The day I enlightened the organization as to the dynamics of the program they sat in shock. I told them outstanding Bulletgrams would be rewarded through the use of a golden bullet. The bullets would be presented at a daily award ceremony and would then be affixed to their individual partition. They would reside there until the end of the year. With each success came lunch on me. If anyone received twenty-five golden bullets, they would be ordained into the Golden Bullet

Club. At the end of the year, the first six individuals to make the club would be flown to Boston, for an all-expenses-paid weekend and award dinner.

On the other hand, unsatisfactory bullets would mandate a different response. As I covered the actions that addressed Ego and Gain you could see a number of Thoroughbreds getting excited. They could already taste those Ipswich clams.

Unfortunately, the majority fell into the Whipped Dog category. I could sense their fear, as they contemplated a partition with no bullets. What would my response be to an unsatisfactory Bulletgram? I explained they had control over their actions and if they chose not to be responsive to their customers, I'm sure I would hear about it. If I received a negative bullet they would have to explain it to me. I told them if anyone received five negative bullets it would be advisable to plan on retiring elsewhere.

You could hear a pin drop. I adjourned the meeting by saying I couldn't wait to start hanging golden bullets. Needless to say, the WD's perception of the program differed from mine. What they didn't know is I controlled the environment.

If a negative bullet came in on someone I knew was doing an excellent job, I would trash it. I knew those would be few and far between. Most people love to recognize effort and only under the worst conditions will they expose nonperformance. I felt confident the vast majority of the bullets coming in would identify people who had excelled.

Four days after my letter and cards went out, I sat anxiously awaiting feedback. The first Bulletgram came in from Des Moines, Iowa. I was a little surprised by the name at the top — Steve Sullivan. In the unsatisfactory block sat a big red X. Under comments, it stated, "This program is shit and so are you."— Unsigned. I threw it out when I rationalized it had been sent by the mother of a WD.

The next day I received a four-page, very articulate analysis from a customer who I respected and I knew had been a fan of mine. He had heard me give a speech about the importance of the human resource and thought this program violated what I had presented. His letter was accurate based upon his perception, but grossly inaccurate as to the assumptions he made about my intent. For the first time I started to have doubts about my pride and joy.

I didn't sleep that night and wondered how I could have been so wrong. As it turned out, my instincts were correct. The next day we received over fifty Bulletgrams and ninety-eight percent were Golden. As individuals were called into the conference room and recognized for their performance, you could feel an energy transformation.

Within a couple months, it became general knowledge around the industry that IP's service had taken a dramatic leap forward. A year later, when the Advisory Council met, customer service was no longer an issue. The council even proclaimed it as one of the company's strengths.

Whenever I'm involved in a success, my first inclination is to take some credit. Then as I review the merits of my contribution, I usually have to give it back. In this particular case all I did was give people a reason to perform. Once they got up to speed, they were on their way. Their ability made them what they ultimately became. I did nothing beyond what my job description mandated.

In leading Thoroughbreds and Rookies, my responsibility seldom transcends that of a street sweeper. Keep the pathway clear and they will meet every challenge. The Whipped Dogs require a bit more attention. No matter how clean the environment is, they will find a way to trip over their emotional baggage. When people suffer from fear, doubt, lack of ability or low self esteem, they barely have enough energy to pick up the pole, much less get over the bar.

When I was more naive, I thought getting a WD to accept my challenge required nothing more than a request. Now that I understand the enervating impact of insecurity, I recognize no major energy will be created until a psychiatric work order has been completed. Feeling good about oneself is important. That occurs much quicker with some kind of achievement.

If Mary is incapable of working the FAX one day, and the next day she can, you have a legitimate success. She'll be excited about her accomplishment. If you tell her "great job," she'll feel even better. When you run it up the flagpole you'll generate some real energy.

I don't know of any leader that doesn't want to have achievement put up in lights. Even though it manifests itself in different ways: bullets on a partition, medals on a uniform or tomahawks on a football helmet — the motive behind the action is always the same: extend the shelf life of a success. A pat on the back, washes away with the next morning's shower.

When you recognize performance in a more lasting, individually specific way, you generate energy every time the recipient is reminded of the event.

A letter of commendation is nice, but a plaque in the foyer makes everyone aware someone is performing. When success is made public, others can become part of the confidence-building program. I've found people like to recognize achievement. They can't do it if they are unaware of its existence.

It also helps in building the team. If Mary can do more, someone else may have to do less. As they thank her for her effort, more energy is created. She's on a high. Praise and Recognition are an emotional narcotic. Mary likes the feeling. Is it surprising she wants to have it again? The next morning, when you arrive bright and early, she asks if she can run the printer. If you think she can, let her. If not, have her turn on the copier. What's important is you reward her ambition with another success. When you do you've started to create a self-fulfilling prophesy. Mary is beginning to believe in her ability. Now, she wants a shot at the computer.

This is where you start to earn your pay. No Whipped Dog should ever be allowed to attempt something that will lead to failure. One step forward and one step back nets out as no gain. Their input, plus your capability analysis will determine the placement of the MAPP. As their psychological orientation transforms itself from one of insecurity to confidence, the way you lead them will change also.

I personally have found nothing more satisfying than rebuilding egos. Not only do I benefit emotionally, but when a 20-percenter starts to perform at 60 percent due to newly acquired confidence, the corresponding 200-percent improvement always gives me a payday.

PASS THE
POTATOES

*Happiness exists not in what
we have, but in the fewness
of our wants.
— Robert Croft*

The alert came, no differently than it had on twenty six previous occasions. When the jumpmaster held up his hand, I knew exactly how much time remained. It would start with a series of jump commands, and end with me hanging 1,200 feet in the air.

GET READY initiated the action of boots stomping on metal flooring. In the dimly lit belly of a C-130 transport plane, the action had a specific purpose. It brought one from a state of reflective contemplation to piercing mental acuity. Gone were thoughts of anything that transcended present time and place. I was awake!

Looking around I couldn't help but be impacted by what I saw. Sitting in the cargo bay, enshrouded by the reddish luminescence of the interior lights, sat forty individuals who were about to put their life in jeopardy. Thunderous engines, 152 MPH winds, and the frigid night air that characterized the environment outside the plane were in stark contrast to the quiet efficiency going on within.

On this jump, there were lots of reasons to be afraid: mountainous terrain, a water hazard, marginal wind conditions and a short drop zone. On the other hand, I'd been properly trained, had twenty-six previous successes and had a bunch of great guys behind me.

STAND UP came next. Without hesitation, we rose in unison. A 180-degree turn and we were ready for the next command.

HOOK UP meant the time had come to secure the static line to guide wire.

CHECK STATIC LINE mandated I inspect the cord that served as my lifeline.

CHECK EQUIPMENT ensured the eighty pounds of sundries I carried had been properly secured.

I waited to receive the final two commands. The first came when the warning light, next to the jump door, illuminated red.

STAND IN THE DOOR dictated there would be no turning back. In sixty seconds, I would be on my way.

GO ordered the stampede to begin. Without hesitation, I and thirty-nine others dove into blackness.

Over the years, I've reflected back on that night jump many times. Sitting in a bar telling war stories, I always highlighted the backbone needed to take that first big step. It's not that I like lying, I just took an oath when I graduated from jump school that I wouldn't tell the truth in public. Everyone who is Airborne knows if you exaggerate the level of bravery it takes to exit an airplane, by association you will come across as a very intrepid individual. People buy drinks for guys with guts.

Relaxing in the privacy of my home, I'll be more candid. If someone asks what part courage played in getting out the door, I've had to admit, none! Courage is the ability to overcome fear. There was no fear involved. The confidence that exists as a result of a paratrooper's preparation is so great, there is no room for fear. But, as important as confidence is in getting someone to accept a challenge, it pales in comparison to the energizing effect of trust.

Confidence got me in the plane, trust got me out of it. I trusted the riggers who packed my chute, the pathfinders that marked the drop zone, the jumpmaster who issued the commands, and the pilot that got us in position. Trust enabled me to put my life in someone else's hands, and when I did, I had no reservations.

TRUST

In my life I have found nothing of greater worth! It is the glue that binds husband to wife, father to daughter, teacher to student and leader to follower. Feelings of trust underlie the Declaration of Independence, the Constitution of the United States and the Bill of Rights. Without Trust there would be no monetary system. Trust enabled David to challenge

Goliath, Lindbergh to assault the Atlantic and six hundred to ride into the valley of death.

I hold trust in such high esteem I will not diminish it with a definition. Trust is not about words. Its genesis is the result of deeds. Whether they be small and insignificant or big and brazen, when you communicate to those you lead, "I am doing my best on your behalf," it is only a matter of time until trust takes you to new heights.

Trust me! Do yourself a favor and never make the request. Because individuals have been known to give their life for someone they trust, they'd rather you not ask for it. They want you to earn it through consistent, credible behavior over time.

To this day, I know a lot of people who still don't fathom how trust is built. Most of them fall into the "exclusivist" category. On any given day, they are magnificent in their ability to measure up. Without hesitation, on Monday, Wednesday and Friday, they can be trusted. The other four days are a different matter. Tuesday they cave in to pressure, Thursday greed, Saturday laziness and Sunday, they just don't give a damn. Tomorrow they'll be back on track.

What they don't understand is trust doesn't evolve when someone is the object of a psychological roller coaster. Hot and cold, wet and dry, in and out and on and off does not exemplify the kind of behavior people grow to trust. As it should be, you are not entitled to be trusted until you have proven yourself over a number of cycles.

I've been told by some I've led, they would follow me, if not to the gates of hell, at least to the outskirts of Newark. If they do, it is only because I have gained their trust. Through thick or thin, good or bad, balmy or bleak, I'm proud to claim I am consistent in my behavior when leading others. I have not and will not succumb to anything that would betray the trust they have placed in my leadership. To do so would violate the sanctity of the relationship, and undermine a fundamental tenet: Leaders can be trusted.

To tell you building trust is easy would be a misrepresentation of the facts. It requires diligence, courage, foresight and a never-ending commitment to the welfare of your team. But because of its bipartisan nature, when you have proven to them you can be trusted, you may rightfully assume they can be trusted.

Early on, I used to ask people what I had to give to earn their trust. I no longer pose the question. After two decades of answers, I finally figured it out. While there are variations on the theme, by and large, when three ingredients are present, the recipe for trust is complete. Not surprisingly they want the same things as you and I: Respect, Support and Reward.

RESPECT

Songs have been sung about it, people killed for it and empires built on it. I've never met anyone that didn't want Respect. Given its unchallenged importance in our lives, why is it absent in so many organizations? It's not as if respect is some abstruse entity. Ask a corporate executive or a tenth-grade drug-dealing dropout to define respect, and I'll wager their answers will be similar.

While the dictionary provides a number of definitions, their synthesis centers on three words. There it is again, The Golden Rule. If you have some questions on the issue, pull up the Universal Energy Chart. Everything listed under Combustion exhibits respect, while each behavioral act beneath Contamination communicates an opposite message.

A while back we established that leaders are in the business of accommodating followers' needs. It seems logical if people require respect, it would be in your best interest to give it. If you are thinking they need to earn it, you're right. I think, if they are doing enough to still be on your team, they have.

SUPPORT

It manifests itself in different ways: emotional, financial, personal or educational. When you entreat someone to raise their MAPP, you are asking them to do more. It seems reasonable if they need a little assistance you should give it.

Making people smarter might mean they may have to go back to school. Greater responsiveness could require a hard-to-come-by capital appropriation. I'll be the first to admit when I'm getting ready to leave the office after a long day and face a two hour commute, I have no desire to be delayed. When Marilyn comes up and says I need to talk to you, I would like to say "later." If I did, I'd be betraying a trust. Leadership isn't about convenience. If you didn't know it, you have an obligation to serve. They trust you'll be there when they need you. Not every request someone makes is going to be easy to accommodate, but whatever investment you make up front will be returned in myriad ways when their actions proclaim, "thanks for the support."

REWARD

Recently, sitting at a dinner table with a number of executives the subject of leadership came up. As various individuals discussed their feelings on the issue, one participant mentioned how she rewarded performance. When she concluded, another sarcastically retorted, "I reward performance every two weeks with a paycheck."

I knew nothing about the antagonist so I couldn't tell whether he was trying to be controversial or actually believed that paying a salary fulfilled his leadership responsibility. If you aren't aware of it, salaries are for doing your job. Rewards are a way of thanking someone for the risk they take in getting to a higher MAPP.

I'll be the first to admit there are people that don't see it my way. Frequently, when the issue of Rewarding performance comes up, the conversation gets pretty heated. Because most organizations have limited resources, not everyone will receive what they think is appropriate. I'm not going to get into a who, what, when, where, why and how discussion, because rewarding performance has much to do with circumstance and environment.

I will say that anyone who is part of a team deserves to be rewarded, in direct relationship to their contribution. When I talk reward I don't necessarily mean monetary compensation. Certainly it is one kind of reward, but experts on the subject have proven that financial rewards are highly overrated.

I define a reward as: anything that makes a statement that you appreciate a person's effort. Rewards come in countless ways. Some are tangible: a pool table in the lunchroom, a pizza party, a plaque on the wall or a promotion. Many are intangible: exposure, latitude responsibility, autonomy, authority or time off to attend a funeral.

Because any reward's value rests in the eyes of the recipient, it is not unreasonable to expect if you reward blindly, you may miss the target. Don't be afraid to ask people what they would like as their reward. You may find out it's not an ashtray with the corporate logo.

Earlier I stated if people were Respected, Supported and Rewarded properly, you would have the necessary ingredients to build Trust. I'll stand on that statement, but I need to modify it. Because we live in a world where individuals are constantly measuring themselves against others, our recipe for Trust is incomplete until we add a measure of fairness. As with success, it lies in the eyes of the beholder. But, unlike success, it is not an energizing agent. Because it is understood fairness is to exist in any leader/follower relationship, when it does you have only done what is expected.

On the other hand, when it's absent, you have a potentially incapacitating problem. If you are looking for others to pledge allegiance to your flag, ensuring everyone is treated fairly becomes a mandate.

I think fairness is a word we should define.

FAIRNESS

- Just and honest.

- According to the rules.

- Adherence to a standard of rightness.

- Impartial and unbiased.

There doesn't appear to be anything cryptic in the definition. Even so, when it comes to fairness, many a leader has gotten into trouble. This is not because they weren't predisposed to being fair, but had more to do with understanding its convoluted nature.

While much about fairness has to do with here and now, substantially more focuses on past and future. When legislating fairness, absolutism does not exist. Fairness is about relativity. It patrols the organization in search of associational interplay. Frank couldn't have been happier about his new office until he found out it was twenty-square-feet smaller than the one they gave to Charlotte.

Certainly one of the major joys in leading involves rewarding performance. How it is done can have a dramatic impact on building trust. Unfortunately, oftentimes a leader's desire to reward is hindered by the callous indifference or bureaucratic bungling of a third party.

Mary Ann had no problem with her pay raise being delayed until she heard Donald's wasn't.

KISS CLINT FOR ME

I received the news from the human resources department that the pay raise I had put in for Mary Ann had been misplaced. In the interim, the corporation had declared a six-month salary freeze. Because her situation had not been acted upon, she fell under the new guidelines. I didn't accept the logic and raised hell. It did no good. I was dealing with a bureaucracy that made Washington look like an entrepreneurship.

I called her into my office and broke the news. You could feel her energy dissipating. When I finished, I told her she would lose around $1,200 because of the error. I then asked her if she planned on taking a vacation that year. She said she had thought about going to Carmel. I then explained I wanted to send her there on a business trip. The company would absorb all expenses up to $1,200. The only thing she had to do, when she returned, was give me a report on whether the area was suitable for a meeting. The look on her face told me she thought my idea was a good one. Mighty fair indeed!

I suspect, if I offered to pick up the tab at her local pub, it would have had almost the same impact. You see, even though people will judge you based upon an end result, their view can be swayed by inclination. If people believe you are trying to do what's fair, you may not energize the situation, but you won't incapacitate it either. Throwing up your hands proclaiming, "It's not my fault" is no way to engender an impression you are in control.

Whether someone views you as fair or not will come as much from how you react to their input, as it will from what you actually accomplish. Did I ever tell you, people are pretty fair.

WHERE'S THE
SHERIFF

A pint of sweat will save a gallon of blood.
— George Patton

Look in the mirror! I hope you didn't think polic-
ing your environment could be delegated. If you did,
I can sympathize with you. Leading is about caring
for others. If I'm going to err, I like to do it on the side
of humanism.

I've never had the desire to wear a black hat. If I
thought I had potential for getting someone back on
track, I would exhaust every possibility. In theory it
sounds great. Experience has taught me differently.
Periodically, due to circumstances beyond my control,
individuals have surfaced who didn't want to hold up
their end of the agreement. Leadership is a two-way
street. If you thought your reward for being on call

twenty-four hours a day was a slap in the face, maybe it's time you started to take up . . . Following.

I've spent ten chapters discussing a leader's responsibility. Nowhere in them did you have to read between the lines. I think my message is clear. I want you to bust your hump for those you lead. Once you have, I don't think it's unreasonable for you to expect something in return. When it isn't provided, you've been shortchanged.

Here's the issue. The contract states: the leader is responsible for accomplishment. The Thoroughbreds are at 19' 4", the Rookies 14' 3" and if Reginald can't cut his MAPP at 11', the objective won't be realized. All of a sudden, an individual situation undermines group enterprise.

There is nothing unreasonable in you requesting the members of your organization, develop skills, meet their responsibilities, assist team members, respond to threats and resolve problems. In short, if they choose to stay around, they have obligations.

If people don't measure up, you have a call to make. It starts with a question. Is Max deficient because he can't or won't elevate his MAPP? If it's the latter, your job is to administer justice.

I'm not talking about a ruler across the knuckles or organizational house arrest. It may have worked for Matt Dillon a century ago, but in today's environment a maladjusted miscreant can do a lot of damage in a fortnight. While you are preparing to read them their Miranda rights, another one of their abusive phone calls just cost you your best account.

Lucky Luciano had the right idea. He used to tell people who betrayed him, "I'm going to cut your heart out with a spoon." Doctor L. made a perfect diagnosis. He knew he had a cancer in his midst. He understood he needed to remove it before it spread its contaminating effects.

It may sound harsh, but it has to be done! The fact is, there are those who will have no remorse if your organization slides into the abyss. They've made no investment and will suffer no loss. It took me a while to figure out why Whipped Dogs do what they do.

For years I thought their never-ending dissatisfaction was a manifestation of true conviction. Claims of mistreatment, lack of support, an incompetent supporting cast, favoritism or a host of other pot stirring allegations were valid. I realize now it's part of their shtick.

Individuals who want to accomplish something find more productive ways of addressing deficiencies. The naysayers tend to have an ulterior motive. Somewhere in their evolution, something went haywire. They now believe the way to get ahead is to destroy everything around them. Their twisted logic has engendered a belief when the organization lies in ashes, somehow they will rise like a phoenix.

I now stand guard, waiting for these individuals to expose themselves. I catch them with help from Shakespeare. I pull out my W-Dogometer and when it registers, "Thou Protesteth Too Much," I ask for a scalpel.

"TOO TUFF" TOMMY

He handles his problems a different way. I've spent my life in gyms across the world and started to believe they were all about the same. That was, until I stumbled into Tommy Ferrentino's place in Tucson, Arizona.

The second I walked through the door of his World Gym, something told me it was different. Although he is the owner and a champion bodybuilder, he can usually be found at the front desk greeting his members. In my case, I wasn't one, but that didn't affect his enthusiasm.

He asked me what I wanted to do and I responded, "Pump a little iron." He replied, "Little iron was on vacation." The challenge had been issued. Although I'm well beyond my "big iron" days, my ego wouldn't allow me to go down the street to the YWCA. "Okay," I said, "bring it on."

The next two hours I suffered immensely. When I collapsed after a set of toe presses, he finally agreed we were finished. While you can't help but be impressed with Tommy's devotion to his members, something far more important underlies what is transpiring in his gym. It has nothing to do with state-of-the-art equipment, a great sound system or surgical cleanliness. It centers around attitude . . . his and theirs.

As he subsequently explained it to me, he has four thousand members. He wants every one of them to be happy. If procedures aren't obeyed, things get screwed up. He stated, compliance is nonnegotiable. The rules are simple. Monopolize a piece of equipment and you get pistol-whipped. Leave a barbell on the floor, and you become dinner for one of his Rottweilers. Spit in the urinal and . . . just don't spit in the urinal!

Controlling the environment enabled Tommy to take a run-down, bankrupt gym operation and turn it into what just received recognition as the best in North America. In a world that continues to move toward

anarchy, Ferrentino's down-home southwestern dicta-
torship works just fine.

AN AVIAN TOUR DE FORCE

Actually the miniseries had nothing to do with birds.
It's easy to get fooled by a title. This masterpiece
showcased life, death, love, commitment, loyalty,
challenge, fairness and trust. *Lonesome Dove*, in my
opinion, the finest movie ever made, was about
Leadership. I shouldn't bring it to your attention
because it delivers the same message as *Leading at
Mach 2*, but with better music.

While I could probably write a book on the intended
meaning of each night's episode, at this juncture in my
dissertation, I'm only interested in the events surrounding the segment on horse rustling. Excuse me,
make that accountability.

Augustus McCrae and Woodrow Call had finally
tracked down the bad guys who had been robbing,
killing and burning sodbusters. When they came
across the group, much to their surprise, they found
their good friend, Jake Spoon, present.

They'd spent a decade as Texas Rangers with Spoon,
and their feelings ran deep. Unfortunately for him,
their commitment to justice ran even deeper. He
pleaded his case by stating he had linked up with the
scoundrels as a means of getting through dangerous
territory. He explained he had not been a perpetrator
in any of the acts, and proclaimed his innocence.

While both of them believed Spoon told the truth, the
fact still remained, *he crossed the line.* As Spoon sat with
neck in noose, you could feel him processing that

input. Suddenly, he kicked his horse and hung himself.

Initially, when I saw the show, I interpreted his decision as an act of love for his friends. He didn't want them to live with guilt. In retrospect, I'm now of the opinion, he did it for himself. Neither of the two would have had any sleepless nights. For all their feeling for Spoon, it held no relevance. The fact was, *he crossed the line.*

As tough as it is to hold people accountable, whenever I start to have doubts about what course of action to take, I try to remember, **justice helps equalize the impact of wrongful behavior**. What you might find encouraging is when justice needs to be dispensed, it is often the result of self-adjudication.

TAKEN TO THE EXTREME

One day, while driving down the main supply route in Korea, I encountered a military vehicle that had crossed the divider and hit a taxi head-on. The passengers in the cab were killed as a result of the collision, but the Korean corporal, lying beside his truck, had met his maker under different circumstances.

When I inquired about what happened, the translated message was, when the drunken soldier realized what his act of irresponsibility had wrought, he became a self-appointed judge, jury and executioner. He put a bullet through his brain.

While his statement of remorse took the harshest

form, the motivation behind it is not novel. You'll find more often than not, if you have led people fairly, they will police their own actions. I think it has something to do with Homo Erectus having . . . a conscience.

When addressing nonperformance, if the best-case scenario doesn't kick in, I have no qualms about operating. The sooner the cancer is removed, the quicker the patient will be on the road to recovery. In most cases, I don't have to chase the disease. When it comes to being held accountable, people may not want it, but they expect it.

ONE GRAM TOO MANY

A. G. knows what I mean. When the bullet program made its debut, a number of dissatisfied customers decided to hold her accountable. Within no time, she had received three unsatisfactory bullets. On the day the fourth arrived, she came and told me it was obvious she was in the wrong job and decided to give notice.

We knew A. G. had been a substandard performer for years, but her file was filled with satisfactory evaluations. Had she not conducted a conscientious self-assessment and then responded accordingly, it would have taken an act of God to remove her. In the interim a lot of innocent bystanders would have suffered.

When people choose to follow someone, I'm convinced they are looking for their leader to safeguard their future. I take my responsibility seriously. I believe Florence Underwood's conscientious effort to help me achieve my goals comes with an expectation. I think, as she gives, she expects to receive. If I give a nonperformer immunity, and that person's subsequent actions hurts the team's performance, I have betrayed a trust. My decision may have deprived Florence of something she earned. I cannot allow that to happen. When I hold people Accountable, I do it without malice. It's just my way of saying, **I will not allow the majority to be held captive by the few**.

<u>N</u>OTES

BORN OF EXPERIENCE

At the beginning of *Leading at Mach 2*, I claimed I had a passion for Leadership. At the time you may have wondered what I meant. If I've done my job, you now know.

In reviewing what I've written, I think I've accomplished my goal. But proving to you I hold the subject dear was not my intent. My objective from the start transcended nothing beyond helping you in your journey to leadership excellence.

Because it is easy to be prejudiced by one's own creativity, I'm not sure I've assisted you at all. I must admit, my thoughts are 100 percent biased. It comes with something I could not control . . . my life's experience. Even though I believe my message is accurate, I won't risk the possibility that it isn't.

It's for that reason I've enlisted the help of five of the finest leaders this country has to offer. While their names may not have marquee recognition, their leadership accomplishments are worthy of the lights. Each, in his own way, has dedicated his life to those that follow. While I know hundreds of outstanding leaders, the individuals you are about to meet have taken the act of leading to new heights.

Because I am not qualified to instruct any one of them about leadership, they have received no guidelines. When I contacted Bob Pearson, Al Gamper, John Maher, Dana Mead and Sam Sebastiani, I made one request: write about leadership. Before you read what they have to say, let me enlighten you as to who they are.

DANA G. MEAD
Chairman of the Board and CEO, Tenneco Inc.

Acclaimed as one of the more innovative thinkers in American industry, Dana Mead was brought to Tenneco, a $13 billion mega-conglomerate, to orchestrate that company's move into the 21st century. As a result of his leadership, Tenneco has begun a dramatic turnaround. While the list of his accomplishments is too extensive to detail, you can see by this short résumé he has prepared himself to lead: West Point graduate, doctorate in Political Science and Economics from MIT, decorated Army colonel (Vietnam), White House Fellow, tenured professor and board member of National Westminster Bancorp, Cummins Engine Company, Baker Hughes Incorporated and ALCO Standard, Inc.

ALBERT R. GAMPER
President and CEO, The CIT Group, Inc.

Educated at Rutgers and Harvard Business School, his vision has taken CIT to new heights. He leads an organization with assets in excess of $14 billion. Under his leadership, The Group has experienced four consecutive years of record earnings, and current results are the highest in the Corporation's eighty-six-year history. His ability to capitalize on financial opportunities is only exceeded by his overwhelming dedication to the welfare of his employees.

MAJOR GENERAL JOHN J. MAHER
Commanding General, 25th Infantry Division.

A graduate of the University of Georgia and Central Michigan University, General Maher has Bachelor of Science and Master of Arts degrees. In addition, his military education includes the General Staff and Army War College. He has spent the majority of his career in Ranger units, and his leadership accomplishments as a Company, Battalion and Brigade commander border on legend. General Maher's decorations and badges include the Legion of Merit (with two Oak Leaf Clusters), Bronze Star, Meritorious Service Medal (six Awards), Vietnam Cross of Gallantry, Joint Service Commendation Medal, Army Commendation Medal, Combat Infantry Badge, Ranger Tab, Master Parachutist Badge with Combat Star, and Air Assault Badge.

ROBERT L. PEARSON
President and CEO, Lamalie Amrop International

He received a Bachelor of Science in Electrical Engineering from Michigan State University and a Masters in Industrial Management from MIT. Since graduating from college he has held a number of key leadership positions in American industry: Senior Engagement Manager, McKinsey & Company, Vice President Corporate Finance, R.J. Financial Corporation, Executive Director, Russell Reynolds Associates and President, Pearson Inc.

His vision has helped Lamalie Amrop become recognized as one of the premier executive recruiting firms in existence. While Pearson is an outstanding leader in his own right, his exposure to leadership talent worldwide, allows for a perspective on the subject that transcends his own experience.

SAM J. SEBASTIANI
Founder and CEO, Viansa Winery & Italian Marketplace

Carrying one of the most distinguished names in the wine industry, he has taken an inherited predisposition to lead to even greater accomplishment. After leaving the family business, where he served as president, to establish his own label, the speed at which success has come is nothing short of extraordinary. His achievements in the areas of viticulture, enology and wetlands preservation have been highlighted in newspapers, magazines and television worldwide. He holds a Bachelor of Science and MBA from Santa Clara University

BOB PEARSON

My company, Lamalie Amrop International, is one of the leading international executive recruiting firms in the world, with fifty-three offices in thirty-two different countries. We are retained by major international organizations to assist them in finding and attracting the highest quality leadership talent available.

Through successfully conducting literally thousands of searches over the twenty-five years the firm has been in existence, we have learned a great deal about leadership and its attributes. Steve has asked me to give you my thoughts on what I see is needed to lead. In that I believe Steve's book is as comprehensive as any I have read on the subject, I will restrict my remarks to those areas that I have found to be most critical in identifying outstanding leadership talent.

First and foremost, a skill-set every good leader nurtures is the art of communication. Probably the most important act of leadership is to establish a clear and compelling vision for your team and continue to reaffirm that vision through effective communication. Every good leader I have recruited had this ability.

Virtually everything about leadership follows the process of establishing what you want to accomplish and then instituting the appropriate programs to get there. Leaders set objectives and are results-oriented. They continue to direct and motivate their organizations unfailingly. While most leaders have great confidence and are fairly rigid in the methods they employ, I have seldom encountered any that were not willing, if needed, to compromise.

Other personal characteristics of a leader, such as decisiveness, innovation, honesty, integrity and personality, are in my view simply tools to help an individual through the process of leading his or her group to ultimately achieve success. Through extensive and complete surveying of organizational peers, subordinates and in all cases bosses, Lamalie tests thoroughly for this skill in all of our recruiting efforts.

In addition, it has been my experience that leadership can be learned, exactly like any complicated skill. Over the years, I have observed that while some individuals may be more charismatic and more effective public speakers than others, leadership is not necessarily a product of those special qualities.

Even though those attributes are a plus, I have found when individuals have a desire to acquire a skill-set and then hone it through practice, in the end they will become just as effective. The only real difference in a person who leads and one who doesn't is mental predisposition. One took on the job because he wanted to, while the other didn't bother.

Very few people step up to leadership without being frightened. We are by nature afraid of making fools of ourselves, of people not responding to our lead, of being wrong about where we are taking our organization. However, I have seen that it's only through trying, sometimes failing, and starting again that one becomes an effective leader. Therefore, another desirable characteristic I look for in leaders is a track record indicating a tendency to be decisive, take prudent risks and be right more often than not. Key accomplishments are easily documented.

In short then, it has been my experience that while most good leaders exhibit some personal characteristics that tend to stand out, what is more important is that they have a commitment to what they are doing, and a willingness to act. They must have the courage to make mistakes, learn from them and continue to pursue their vision until it becomes a reality.

AL GAMPER

Some people believe that leadership is instinctive. I could accept that, I guess, if it is also acceptable to say that instinct can be shaped by experience.

In my opinion, one of the most useful and critical attributes of a good leader is the ability to learn. I'm convinced that experience — learning from others, observing the "masters at work," making and correcting mistakes along the way — contributes greatly to one's knowledge bank and helps shape one's instincts. Those instincts are also influenced by personal values, ideals, desires, motivations, likes, dislikes and a host of other factors. The budding leader sharpens his or her leadership skills by learning at an early age how to identify role models and how to take advantage of what those individuals have to offer.

Leaders come in all shapes and sizes, and while we may detect different personalities, purpose and strength in those we think of as leaders, we can usually agree on who is a leader when we meet one. Good leaders have certain common characteristics.

As I see it, there are two very broad categories of leaders: those who lead for a short time in business, government or civic capacities (I call them the "Sprinters"), and those who affect change — take charge — for long periods of time ("the Marathoners").

There is a distinction as well between managers and leaders. Managers can be "Sprinters," short-term leaders, but their primary purpose is to administer or supervise. The "Marathoner" has a long-term commitment to effecting change, to instilling purpose in an organization and its members. This is the group that I have always found intriguing.

Nothing has meant more to me in my career than having been in the company of several "Marathoners" from whom I could absorb management styles, practices and methods. Three men, in particular, served as mentors for me at different stages of my career, and if I am deemed a leader today, it can be attributed to the fact that I learned all I could from each of these men.

Mentoring is a critical element of the leadership-development process that is often underestimated. It can be as subtle as a priest taking aside a high school student and convincing him of the importance of community service, or it can be as explicit as a special part of a management-training program at a large corporation.

The three men who influenced me were all leaders in their own right, but each taught me a different lesson. The first was a gentlemen of great charm, character and distinction. His name was George Moran. George was one of those individuals who inspired one to automatically put a "Mr." in front of his name. It took me about five years before I could comfortably address him as just "George."

He had the uncanny ability to identify the true potential in people — and he could predict the next generation of leaders within our organization, work with them and nurture them. He was a risk taker, willing to challenge the conventional wisdom even when doing so might have been career threatening. Trying something new, being the first to do things, he exhibited a boldness and candor that matched in strength his gregarious and warm nature. I watched him with admiration — and I learned from him.

Later in my career, I crossed paths with a very different, yet equally influential mentor. Cool, intellectual and almost a bit ascetic in character, Edward Farley was a man who could be consumed by detail yet broad in perspective — a leader who was resolute in his convictions. He was a formidable teacher with a work ethic that would shame an Amish farmer.

His mentoring brought home the importance of standards, values and candor in dealing with others. He also taught the necessity of taking on a task with the energy and willingness to get totally immersed in it. His foe was superficiality, his friend was detail. "God is in the detail" would be an apt plaque for his office wall.

The third person who had an enduring influence on me was John McGillicuddy, the leader of one of the largest banks in the United States. Anyone who knows John knows him as strong-willed and compassionate, a man of keen intellect and dogged determination.

He would always point out the importance of "talking things out" when critical decisions needed to be made. What a great idea — to avoid impulsive decisions while hearing all sides of the argument. He had the patience of Job and always let others express their opinions on business matters.

Beyond just patience and understanding, perhaps John McGillicuddy's greatest contribution to my development as a business leader was the deep conviction that the people of an organization are the organization; that building the spirit and attitude of a company is as important as building its balance sheet and income statements. He taught that motivating, rewarding and creating a nourishing environment is essential to an effective organization—and, that to achieve that level of cooperation, a leader must not be aloof, distant or disinterested. Management must be participative, and top management must be involved.

You could find no better example of an involved leader than John McGillicuddy. His involvement in his business spilled over into his involvement in his community, both as a business leader and as a concerned citizen, and this lesson was well received.

I found that aspect of his leadership particularly inspirational and am proud to say that I have always tried to inspire and encourage a deep sense of community involvement among CIT employees. John McGillicuddy helped convince me that successful companies, and successful individuals, should give something back to their communities, and that there is a strong correlation between companies that achieve superior results and companies that commit time, energy and, in some cases, money, to important causes. The people at CIT surely believe that — more than two-thirds of our employee population volunteers time and energy to worthy community organizations.

To have been exposed to these three leaders was a great experience for me. From one I learned about taking risks and bringing a creative eye to my role. From another I learned about the importance of standards, candor and paying attention to details. And from a third I learned about the importance of people to an organizations's growth and success. From all of them I learned about leadership in what can only be described as a "real world" laboratory.

As I said earlier, mentoring is a critical and often overlooked element in the leadership development process. But it is not the only critical element. Another very important factor is the home environment—the influence a family and its circumstances can have on the development of a leader.

When I was young, my family had great difficulty dealing with the financial strain caused by serious medical problems. As a family, we were required to "pull together" for a common cause — not unlike the belt-tightening and cooperation that takes place at the corporate level during challenging times — and make sacrifices to survive.

Because of my early experience, one of my strongest inclinations is to provide a safety net for troubled employees — employees who may be in financial need, those who need special counseling from trained professionals or those who might be experiencing a variety of family troubles.

There are lessons to be learned in every experience and, for me, there was much to learn in dealing with real financial uncertainty. This early experience was helpful in directing me toward building a corporate environment with the same degree of spirit, cooperation and loyalty.

"Loyalty"—is a word that is more likely to invoke argument today than it is to conjure up a pleasant image. Business leaders today complain about the lack of a loyal workforce, but it is my contention that a business leader should work to create loyalty — it's not a given, it must be earned.

In a business environment replete with restructurings, mass firings and organizational upheaval— caused by poor management decisions in the first place—how can a business leader expect loyalty from his employees without first taking a good share of the responsibility for the conditions that caused this climate of unrest? The common perception at the employee level is that management and the corporate leadership doesn't care — bad management decisions are corrected and maybe even erased by restructuring and layoffs. That behavior doesn't promote loyalty, it promotes insecurity and mistrust.

I am convinced that one way to earn the loyalty of those who work for you is to provide employees with attractive, meaningful benefits, safety nets and a comfortable but challenging work environment. Leadership demands that loyalty be encouraged and nurtured through real acts, not wordy speeches or memos.

When I think about loyalty, I am reminded of my experience in the Marine Corps, an organization that prides itself on the highest degree of loyalty. It was my observation that the loudmouth, "macho" types could never hope to get the level of respect from their men as did those who led by example. The leaders who asked no more from their men than they did from themselves — and in whose eyes you could always read genuine concern — were the officers who exhibited true leadership and who were rewarded by the loyalty of those that followed them.

For me, leadership is evolutionary. Those of us who are privileged to be in positions of leadership have a great responsibility to the people we lead. It is a day-in, day-out process — lessons continue to be learned, mistakes continue to be made, growth continues to occur. I think it may have been Ernest Hemingway who was once asked how he could be so spontaneous in his writing. His classic Hemingwayesque response went something like, "I write everything three or four times."

There is no shortcut to effective leadership. It is a condition that continues to change. The good leader recognizes it as a fluid, dynamic learning process — in short, a work in progress.

JOHN MAHER

As a rule, I shy away from saying or writing any-thing about personal achievements because anything a leader accomplishes in the military is done through other people, as a member of a team.

To keep the record straight, I still strongly believe that, but Steve hooked me with the passions he described at the beginning of his book. Like him, I'm also passionate about the subject of leadership and therefore have a few remarks I hope you find appropriate.

I take this opportunity to write about leadership as a form of payback to those officers and noncommis-sioned officers who not only trained me and provided an unfailing leadership example, but also inspired me to accomplish what I have, in service to my country and the U.S. Army.

When I reflect on my career and those leaders that had the greatest influence, I go back to my return from Vietnam in 1973. Still a lieutenant, I joined the rebuilding 101st Airborne Division at Ft. Cambell, Kentucky. Reforming a company is tough enough by itself, but when you throw in the additional factors of low morale, a slashed military budget, a new "all-volunteer" force in a downsizing Army and few remaining professional noncommissioned officers, the challenges become even greater.

My unit had its share of problems and I initially had some concerns about my battalion commander. I won-dered why he was so slow in making, what should have been, easy decisions. He never failed to ask his people, in many cases individuals at the lowest level, for their opinions.

I thought it had to do with indecisiveness. As it turned out, he was a master psychologist. His participative leadership style not only got everyone involved, but it made them feel a part of the team. Individually, he encouraged each of us to hold up our responsibility.

What I couldn't appreciate at the time, but I do now, is much of what he did went against his natural incli-

nation. It would have been easy for him to make quick independent decisions, but he realized teams are built through cooperative effort. As he encouraged participation, he developed each and every one of us. As we grew, the battalion went on to become one of the very best 700-man organizations in the entire 18,000 man division. The difference between us and the other units was simply: Leadership.

My association continued when I became a battalion commander and he returned as my commanding general. I watched him lead the entire division with the same principles I had witnessed earlier in my career. He developed the team with his own positive example and demonstrated genuine concern for all his subordinates. He convinced them they were the world's experts at what they did. He not only took care of them but also implemented programs that supported their families. He developed an environment of respect and loyalty. No one wanted to let him down and everyone wanted to meet or exceed expectations. Under his leadership the 101st Airborne Division regained its stature as the best the Army had to offer.

On a more personal note, he developed me through coaching and counseling. He never failed to address any shortcoming or acknowledge any success. In addition, he selflessly encouraged me to leave his unit, to pursue an early command opportunity. He sponsored me unfailingly and pushed me toward success.

Thoughts of the many possible vignettes of success I might share bring back great memories. There were common threads in all my commands. We were proud, caring, resourceful, resilient and never failed in accomplishing our mission (by no means at the expense of a sister unit).

I believe a leader's role is to help team members succeed, and I am proud of the successes many of my former subordinates have enjoyed. An additional pay-back comes from observing the high performance of their units.

Since the majority of my career has revolved around leadership assignments, I would like to share some of what I have learned about leading. Today, when I speak at various military leadership training pro-grams, I generally frame my remarks around, "taking charge, communicating, motivating and being dedi-cated." Here are my thoughts on each.

Taking Charge — When you are put in charge of something, take charge. Even if you get a job you don't want, do it to the very best of your ability. As quickly as possible, determine which direction you need to go or what azimuth you want to follow. When you move out, don't look back.

Communicating — Communicate to your subordi-nates how you like to operate and what is important to you. Make them aware you have faith in their ability and will support them in the execution of their duties. Let them know they will be held accountable to the team for doing their job. Give your subordinates their missions and their tasks, but don't tell them how to do their job. Most importantly, communicate to your sub-ordinates you are aware of their potential and what they are capable of becoming.

Motivating — Challenge your subordinates to meet your high expectations. Be willing to share their hardship. What you do is far more important than what you say. Encourage them to use their initiative and create an environment where they can look forward to their work. Reward their performance at every opportunity.

Being Dedicated — Dedicate yourself to your people and their mission. In the military, it's mission first but people always. Be considerate of and in tune with their needs and those of their families. Put those you lead in the spotlight. Be loyal to them always.

When I'm addressing more senior leadership forums, I share many of the same tips, but I focus on three specific areas of performance.

Be Yourself — Don't change what got you where you are. Anyone can spot a fake. Likewise, everyone recognizes someone who is his or her own person. The original always has more worth.

Take care of your people — Help them with their careers, their needs and their problems. Communicate with them at every opportunity. Never assume they know they are a part of the team. Ensure they understand their contribution is needed.

Trust your instincts — It has taken a lifetime to teach you what you know. As the senior leader in your organization, trust your instincts. Don't turn your back on anything that doesn't seem right. It probably isn't! If you ignore it you will pay a price later.

PERSONAL LEADERSHIP EXPERIENCES

Having had the opportunity to serve with and for some truly outstanding leaders, I have been able to apply lessons learned until "we" got it right. I always focused unit leadership on the elements noted earlier in this section. I learned to establish a command climate in which leaders were encouraged to take the initiative. In doing all of this, I wanted to develop the leadership skills of my subordinates so they would function without me.

Tell them what to do but not how to do it.

Very early in my command of Company B, 2d Ranger Battalion, we had received a training alert and a mission to conduct an airborne assault into Pinyon Canyon, Colorado. I recall working very hard on the details of the plan, trying to develop and synchronize all aspects of the operation. As the planning became increasingly more complex, I asked my experienced executive officer for some advice on how he would handle the assault element. With the steady eyes of a competent combat veteran, he told me in no uncertain words that he would assign the assault mission to one of our platoons, and have them brief me back on how they would execute that assault. How simple! Why would I do anything else? I almost got trapped into personally planning every detail of this "special operation." Needless to say, we came up with logical, well understood plans, and although we faced challenges on the operation (including the loss of our assault platoon leader), the execution by all the platoons was absolutely superb. That was the beginning . . . and what a great lesson to learn: Tell them what to do but not how to do it.

Tell them what you expect of them, and they will rise to the occasion.

Not long after that experience we departed for Panama and annual Jungle Training. The conditions on the deployment were to be particularly difficult.

We would train in virgin forests and would execute all missions in the jungle at night. After a week of operations slashing through thick jungle and failing to meet our mission time lines, my men were getting frustrated at their lack of results even though they were putting out what they thought was a 100 percent.

On our final operaton, we were given what seemed to be a mission impossible. In fact, we had been given thirteen hours to hit our target instead of the intended thirty-seven. The operations staff had mistakenly given us a one-day early hit time. As determination replaced frustration, I gave the platoon leaders their tasks, *and told them what I expected of them!* It was unreasonable, but I convinced them we would accomplish our mission. With lots of luck, ingenuity, determination and skill, our company found its objective on time (one day early) and called in for permission to "hit." Although our higher headquarters thought we had jungle fever, they finally believed that we were miraculously at our objective and allowed us to execute our successful raid. The moral of this story is that people will rise to your expectations if you clearly communcicate what's on your mind.

As the command tour of just over fifteen months continued, we completed sixteen major deployments around the world. In each, the company consistently accomplished its mission, and the leaders continued to grow. As we completed our final training deployment, I turned the company over to my executive officer to command a night amphibious raid.

What a joy it was to watch the company perform as well or better in my absence than when I was at the helm. An even greater joy came as a result of watching the men of that company flourish in their development, contributions, and promotions.

That company has been a lasting point of reference for me. I have tried to lead two battalions and a brigade with the same principles applied at higher echelons. As I left my second battalion command, I looked back with tremendous pride on the battalion's accomplishments. A few months later they led the Panama Invasion in Operation Just Cause, and conducted the airborne assault onto Rio Hatos. They performed superbly.

My reward was when the battalion returned and sergeants passed on to me, "Sir, it was just like our training!" I beamed like a proud father. More importantly, those soldiers (of all ranks) are leading other units in the Army today. Somehow I know that they are all winners; that they will challenge and care for their people, clearly communicate what they want done, and then let their subordinates sort out how it will happen.

So there you have it, a quick summary of what started me ticking, what I think makes others tick, and why I passionately pursue this profession I love.

DANA MEAD

Leadership is highly personal. That mundane "truism" is important at the outset — "to thine own-self be true." A leader must not try to be someone else, nor demand that his or her subordinates do likewise. Unless a leader recognizes this at the outset, the individual's full potential to lead will never be realized. The most devastating observation that can be made of a leader is that "he or she is a phony." When this occurs, the trust, respect, affection and even awe that is so essential between leader and led, will never materialize.

GETTING THE PEOPLE RIGHT

I always begin with the premise that the cardinal task of leadership is to "get the people right." Get the people right and everything else will follow. It is incredible how little time CEOs spend on people, yet the success of an organization is directly proportional to the percentage of time its leaders spend recruiting, developing, nurturing and guiding their leaders. The first principle of leadership I was taught as a plebe at West Point — "know your people and look out for their welfare" — should be engraved in every corporation's head office. I recently read about the CEO of a highly successful major corporation who personally knew the top five hundred managers in his organization — a goal all of us should emulate.

How do you "get the people right"? Very carefully and with great difficulty. I've had the privilege of sitting on the President's Commission on White House

Fellowships for two decades — charged each year with choosing a few of America's "best and brightest" to serve as Fellows. I've personally interviewed over one thousand of this country's most accomplished, best educated, most dedicated young men and women. It has given me a rare insight into young leaders and what sets them apart. My conclusions?

First, character counts for more than anything else. Integrity, courage, balance, persistence, friendliness, confidence and optimism are more important than all the Phi Beta Kappa keys, summas and Heisman's.

Let me bring it down to real life examples. Balance. Here I'm talking about a balance between humility and overweening confidence, in street parlance, between "knowing it all" and realizing that you don't! The customer has suddenly been recognized to be king in American business. One of the best known principles of customer relations is "really listening to the customer." Jack Carew's selling system even uses a nice little acronym to facilitate problem solving: LAER—Listen, Acknowledge, Explore and Respond. People without "balance" can't listen effectively. We all know the person who is smart, aggressive and knows it all. Talking to that kind of person is "a dialogue with the deaf." They can't lead because they can't listen. The concept can be applied across a host of other character traits.

Tenneco is becoming known as a company with talented, aggressive and innovative senior leadership—few, if any, of whom fit the traditional corporate leadership template. Mike Walsh, our late CEO, began his business life as a public defender and also ran a statewide campaign for Common Cause; I have been an Army officer, professor and White House staffer; my senior strategist was a highly sucessful partner of an investment bank; my Chief Financial Officer is an

MIT Ph.D; my senior human resource executive a foundation executive and my general counsel started as a a poverty lawyer. An unlikely crew to sit atop a Fortune 50 company, and to manage one of the country's major industrial transformations. Yet, they all fit one template: people with impeccable character. (Incidentally, there are plenty of Phi Betas, summas and "stars" in this crowd, also.)

MANAGEMENT PRINCIPLES

At Tenneco we have a couple of simple management principles — "Be Fair-minded" and "The Doctrine of No Surprises." These are hardly unique. Many companies have some variation of these, but all of us differ in the way we breathe life into them.

"Be Fair-minded" is often misinterpreted to imply a relaxed tolerance of mistakes or inadequate results. Nothing could be further from the truth. For us, it means understanding that leadership must deal intelligently with the tension between encouraging prudent, even aggressive risk-taking, and the failure that will result part of the time.

I like to translate it simply into, "Don't repeat the same mistake." Volumes have been written about the learning opportunities afforded by mistakes. That's all good, but repeated learning "opportunities" of this kind can be costly and disastrous. Early in my military career I was assigned the "privilege" of being Aide de Camp to a general reputed to be the meanest, toughest man in the U.S. Army. He was! He fired and chewed up Aides at an alarming rate. At the end of my first two months, which I filled with scores of minor and major gaffes (real and imagined), he called me in for a counseling session. I only remember the end of it — and I always will. After reviewing my trial period shortcomings in excruciating detail — numbing detail — he said, "You're the best aide I've ever had, and for just one reason — you never make the same mistake twice." I've tried to take that and apply it to a broader credo of "Be Fair-minded," be tolerant of mistakes once, but be very tough when people are not smart enough or energetic enough to learn from them.

The "Doctrine of No Surprises" permeates all of Tenneco's management systems and leadership processes. While it includes a number of standard operating procedures — early notification, horizontal and lateral communication, and the like—we have put in place formal and informal structures to facilitate compliance. I have tried to take it a bit further — making it a catalyst for the big-time culture shift we are trying to achieve.

We want to identify early on, issues, problems and trends at every level of the organization. For a manager or a shop director to do this takes courage, self-confidence and trust. (You can see how there is rough, holistic approach to leadership here — "Be Fair-minded" is a key to progress.) Our mantra is, "Problems are to be solved, not covered up," and we expect our leaders to live by it. No one gets high marks for informing me about a "big surprise" the weekend before. I'll take the individual who bubbles up and attacks the little surprises before they become major.

Incidentally, we use a lot of third-party polling—

running through and around our management layers to try to plumb the depth and rate of change. This can be very threatening unless an environment of trust has been created. We characterize it as part of the application of the "Doctrine of No Surprises."

A NON-TRADITIONAL VIEW OF EMPOWERMENT

I haven't slipped into using the fashionable term "empowerment" yet, because I don't like the psycho-babble that has surrounded what was once a relatively clean concept — matching authority and information at the right level with action. We take a less traditional view of empowerment at Tenneco.

First, I'm not a believer in the notion that goal setting is a bottom-up exercise — a belief that is very much in vogue in some circles. While I believe goal setting should be a broad interactive process, I've found goals rolled up from below always will be less ambitious and slower than necessary to achieve excellence and create real change. At a recent leadership meeting, I asked my 450 top managers how much "sand" was in their original budget submissions — the answer, no surprise — was that across six businesses the average "sand-bag" was 20 percent! (Experienced CEOs know exactly why this is so because most of them have tried it at some point in their careers.) I have routinely increased both our annual and five-year targets by big-time stretch amounts (taking out the sand and the bag), and each year we have exceeded them! A few years ago a major U.S. company was trumpeting their 6 percent annual improvement in productivity. There was understandable congratulatory rhetoric until they realized that their major offshore competitor was getting 4 percent — a month!

To get substantial improvements in performance, goal-setting has to be done from top-down, not by what in a bottom-up system is essentially done "by committee." Years ago the New Yorker had a cartoon of a father with his son looking up at a monument with four figures on top, and explaining to the son, "There are no great men anymore, just committees!"

STRETCH GOALS

In my book, "great committees" are few and far between. Leadership requires leaders to set goals and to accept accountability for achieving them. We set stretch strategic goals with another very important purpose — to facilitate change. Easily attainable goals contribute to lackadaisical acceptance of the status quo — a comfortable but inevitable recipe for disaster. We set goals that can only be achieved by doing business differently — by changing — and doing it throughout the organization.

I insist — demand — that these stretch goals be cascaded down to the lowest level of every business — so the person in the shop tractor assembly line knows exactly how his or her specific goals fit into the overall picture. For example, we had an annual goal at J. I. Case of eliminating $200 million dollars of failure costs—60 percent of that inside the plants. During a recent visit, one hourly assembler showed me his "chart" on grease-stained tablet paper outlining the

$2,000 of internal failures he was charged with taking out that year. He knew exactly what his mission was, where it fit and that he was accountable.

This is key, in my mind, to real empowerment. He was not told "how" to do this, only what his mission was. He was fully empowered, within reasonable bounds, to figure it out. His leaders were responsible to set the goals, give him the resources, and then stand back.

Empowerment without a clear understanding of what is required is anarchy! Is there anything more frustrating and debilitating to great performance than an organization running around "empowered" without any clear notion of what they are empowered to do? Chaos.

A BIAS TO ACTION

Action. The primary operating value we expect our leaders to exhibit at Tenneco is a bias to action. Placing emphasis on the speed of change, which although it is not the same thing, goes hand in glove with action. We value action more than contemplation. When individuals act, they create opportunities, enhance morale and improve productivity.

How does leadership reinforce this core value? First, by example. Our internal polling at all levels of the organization showed that one of the major impediments to speed is slow decision-making. Once our leaders understood this, they began to clean up their processes — creating improved focus, faster and better information and greater delegation. All of it, reduced the cycle-time in achieving results. (We're not trying to make bad decisions faster!)

Speed and action are also a function of how much time decision-makers have to devote to a specific problem or issue. We have been working very hard to find ways to free up their time — for quality decision-making. For example, we have cut the number of reports to headquarters (always time-consuming) by 75 percent; we've increased the capital approval levels by 100 percent so we are no longer burdened at both ends by small capital approvals; and by virtue of a new shared services construct we'll free up our movers and shakers from supervising hundreds of routine administrative activities that add little or no value, and for which no customer should be paying. This enables our leaders to focus on design and engineering, manufacturing, distribution, sales, marketing and customer service — the core activities for success.

Action and speed also apply to "learning from mistakes." We want speedy assessment of failures so we can prevent the pyramiding of mistakes. Napoleon once observed that in studying battles that, "On the day of battle, naked truths abound, but the next day, they are back in their uniforms and gone." We don't dwell on mistakes, but we do assess them quickly so that we can make corrections and move on.

GETTING RESULTS

Results. Our second core operating value is an unrelenting focus on results. We want results, not best efforts. In my opinion, we have too long rewarded, even celebrated, best efforts, despite failure. How often have you heard a failure complimented for having "given it the old college try"? We accepted the notion that extraneous events, over which we had no control, dictated our ability to succeed or fail.

At Tenneco, we stress that achieving results is in the control of our leadership — that our leaders have a responsibility to lead change, to tackle reality head-on, and despite outside influences, to win. We tell them that we give no credit for "warming up on the sidelines." The big-time practice player who looks so great in Wednesday's scrimmages, but who can't move the ball on Saturday, is not rewarded. If the assumptions in the plan aren't panning out, go back and rework the assumptions, change the plan of attack — but hit the results. Our managers, early on, didn't understand that "the plan," any plan, is simply a baseline for departure from which to make adjustments and improvements, not a set of stone tablets from which no variance is permitted.

This intensive, clenched teeth, hardheaded emphasis on results puts a special, ethical burden on leadership. In this environment, there will always be temptation to cut corners, play the system, push the envelope. Our challenge is to hit world-class results in an ethical, moral, legal and highly professional way, and to convince everyone in the company that it can and will be done that way only.

LEADING CHANGE

Finally how do you lead and assess leaders? All of the foregoing really deals with that subject — but here are a few additional observations.

At Tenneco, the prime criterion for assessing our leaders is how successfully they lead change. This is key because we are undergoing a dramatic and wide-ranging business and cultural transformation.

There are literally hundreds of underlying criteria, but to name a few:

- Is the cultural innovation we expect them to be leading happening fast enough and deep enough?

- Are they hitting stretch targets?

- Are their management processes changing fast enough to support the cultural changes and results they seek?

- Are they recruiting, developing and surrounding themselves with other leaders of change?

On the last point, Machiavelli said you could evaluate a ruler by the princes he surrounded himself with. Real leaders of change are always seeking other leaders of change to assist them. Those who don't are probably talking a much better game than they play.

Speaking of that, we expect our leaders to play the same game they talk. A wise old fellow I once worked for used to insist every office post a slogan that reminded his leaders that "an organization does well only those things the boss checks." Our leaders who proclaim dedication for cost of quality, but who never check it or review it, will not last long.

We value leaders who are tough competitors. We hire people who hate to lose, to be second best. As a result, we lean toward people who either as athletes or students have had to put it on the line in tough competition and been personally accountable for results. I personally like people who have competed in team sports — when they have had to balance their own individual contribution and recognition with the team's success or failure. I also believe I can get a better sense of a leader's true capabilities by getting to know his or her subordinates. Do they reflect the fire, the drive, the enthusiasm, the optimism, the loyalty that I expect to find in their boss?

I also place a lot of emphasis upon what I term "surrogates for management and leadership." While I use a number of these surrogates, safety is a favorite, because I believe a leader who can manage safety successfully can manage anything. At its essence, safety management involves changing behavior; likewise, leadership, at its essence, involves changing behavior. Most safety problems are behavior related, not caused by mechanical or physical shortcomings. Safety performance is also a terrific indicator of employee morale. People daydreaming about either a real or imagined abuse by payroll or the boss tend to get hurt or hurt others. Fellow employees who don't care about each other tend to overlook safety problems and unsafe activities by their colleagues. Safety requires attention to detail. It includes good housekeeping. It requires action and empowerment at every level. In short, good leadership.

Finally, leaders create a sense of excitement and find ways to ignite it in others. During a particularly difficult stage of the Italian campaign in World War II,

General George Patton was approached by his officers who complained about the hardships the soldiers were facing. "What would they rather be doing," Patton asked them, "shoveling manure in Missouri or making history here with the Seventh Army?" Our leaders try to let our people see a broader picture — that we are making business history, in a small way, and encourage them to get excited by the prospect.

RECOGNIZING LEADERSHIP QUALITIES

At the close of the first bonus year at Tenneco, I announced to our senior managers that half of their annual bonuses would be based upon a discretionary judgment by me of their "leadership." There was the anticipated reaction from a group that had always been paid bonuses calculated by a set of rigid financial formulae. How could anyone possibly evaluate anything as "soft" and "incommensurable" as leadership? My answer was, to paraphase a former Justice of the Supreme Court:

"Leadership at Tenneco, to me, is like trying to define pornography. It may be very difficult to define it, but when you see it, you'll know it."

As leaders, we have the responsibility to create the vision, the values, the organizational structure and norms to enhance the performance of great people. Leadership may be difficult to define, but we know that we cannot succeed without it, and that we will certainly recognize it by the exceptional results it produces.

SAM SEBASTIANI

As I slid off the rock into the Stanislaus river a half hour's hike from my family and two hours by horseback from the nearest road, I was given an opportunity to once again struggle for survival. The accident was of my own making. I was attempting to step to a precarious fly-fishing perch when I slipped and fell backward onto the granite embankment. Not only was I knocked semiconscious but when my shoulder encountered a protruding boulder it immediately dislocated with the impact. Fortunately, the freezing temperature of the water brought me to consciousness. The adrenaline that came from fear enabled me to pull myself from the river and struggle back to camp.

After a number of attempts to put my shoulder in place, it was determined I needed a medivac out. Due to some logistical problems, that didn't occur for fifteen hours. While I sat next to the bonfire that illuminated what would serve as the helicopter Landing Zone, I couldn't help but reflect back on other challenges I'd met. While many of them are personal in nature and have significance only to me, there are some that could be of value to anyone studying leadership.

The first real challenge I encountered was in 1980 when my father passed away, leaving the family wine business at a very inopportune time. His unfortunate death put me in a leadership situation that transcended any experience I gained as a student-body president or military officer.

I instantly inherited a disgruntled employee group. For a variety of reasons, they'd been incited to turn against a management philosophy that had enabled

our small business to grow to national prominence, with over three million cases sold in 1980.

What that success did not reveal was a kind of cancer different from what had killed my father. That cancer embodied assumptions and procedures that had made us successful, but no longer worked.

One assumption was, if I provide you with a place to work, you will perform to the best of your ability. A changing world forced me to rethink how I had to attend to my organization. I found through experience, that unspoken contract no longer existed. People wanted more! My challenge then was to give it to them, by changing the way we had historically operated. Without a new direction, either competition or our employees (through no malice) would destroy what had been created.

The first thing that I did, out of intuition, was to build a first-class employee break room with all the amenities. In an environment of distrust, I felt we needed a place for all of us to gather that was common ground. I followed this initial action with a thorough revamping of every workstation. I knew the environment played a key role in productivity. As I was making these changes, a strike was called by the union.

I recognized we had to keep the winery running with management, but I also knew this strike would come to an end and I thought it prudent not to antagonize our labor pool. It didn't take Solomon's wisdom to recognize there was a great potential for confrontation between managers who were breaking sweat for the first time, and employees who were losing pay.

I felt the best way to ameliorate the situation was to get people's minds off the issues at hand. The first morning I went out to the picket line and advised everyone that their black and white signs would not do. I told them they had to be painted in the winery colors.

I provided the paint and brushes and a table for them to use to keep their signs looking vibrant throughout the strike. In addition, we began an early morning donut and coffee run. We took sandwich orders for lunch and had a wine break in the afternoon. It came to me these employees had no desire to strike. They only wanted to resolve their grievances. The more understanding we showed for their plight, the greater their willingness to listen.

It didn't take long to figure out leader and follower both had a role to play in the relationship. I began to realize that management was a two-way street. Somewhere along the way, it came to me that everyone is a manager even if it is only at their work station. If they are given an opportunity to feel responsibility they will more likely be responsible. I was quickly learning that leadership is about allowing others to grow. When they do, you have a more valuable resource. The organization becomes stronger because of it.

Armed with that knowledge it seemed logical we should manage our resource like any valuable commodity. I immediately canvassed the country and found the best human resources director available: Al Graham.

With Al's help and direction we instituted programs that at the time were revolutionary for Sebastiani Vineyards. We told people if they weren't happy with their job and wanted to change, we would try to help them. As a result, the office manager became the warehouse supervisor the supply clerk became a secretary, two wine makers went into public relations and bottling people started to drive forklifts.

Over a five-year period from 1980 to 1985 Sebastiani Vineyards won 272 awards. In the last two years we racked up more recognition for our wines than any winery in America. The organization went from a disorganized and disruptive group, to a focused and deliberate team of people, intent on enjoying their daily work, but doing so with a commitment that allowed us to move to a higher level of performance.

Leadership has its risks! On December 30, 1985, I was fired from my job as president. The reasons are not important. The Chinese word for crisis is opportunity and I had now been given an opportunity of a lifetime. I could carve my own niche.

With the help of my wife, Vicki, a partner, and a few friendly bankers I raised enough capital to start Viansa. Upon completion of the winery and its accompanying bird sanctuary, disaster struck. An earthquake in San Francisco, a lingering recession and the Iraq confrontation destroyed our tourism. Our tasting room and Italian Marketplace were empty. Success now hinged on our ability to get a larger piece of a shrinking pie. The odds were against us and I would have been more frightened but I realized the lessons I'd learned at my former place of employment had taught me well.

My job now was to create an environment that visitors wanted to see and employees would adopt. To that end, I became nothing more than a coach and cheerleader. I described the scene, and our people's efforts made my vision a reality. By giving our employees freedom of moment, encouragement, training and support they have created what Viansa is today.

My father, August, taught me a superior wine is a product of chemistry. Experience has taught me, **a superior organization is a product of people.**

NOTES

EPILOGUE

In memory, lies immortality.
— Luiz Freitas

As I sat waiting, I thought about what his life entailed, since we were together as Ranger Lieutenants. After six years of serving my country, I made the decision to leave the Army, to pursue a bank account. Bob Hoffman, who had always operated on a higher plane, followed a different path. I knew his decision centered on where he thought he could make the biggest contribution.

While Leadership is important everywhere, leading others in life-and-death struggles, takes on even greater significance. Hoffman had decided to make the military a career.

When he walked through the door, his appearance

belied the image created of him in the book, *LRRPS in Vietnam*. Standing before me was a gray-haired, soft spoken, weathered West Pointer who had spent the majority of his working career in precarious situations.

He looked dramatically different than the warrior whose picture hung in the Ranger Hall of Fame. A lot of water had passed under the bridge since we'd been together. As we rehashed old times, the name Harvey Moore came up. I asked how he was doing.

Hoffman didn't immediately answer. When his eyes moistened I realized his thoughts had been teleported to another place and time.

He's dead, he responded. Knowing Sergeant Moore as I did, I expected Hoffman would tell me he died while leading his troops in combat. He didn't. As Hoffman recounted it to me, it happened during a training exercise.

Moore's Battalion Commander needed an RTO (Radio Telephone Operator) to accompany him to one of the outlying command posts. Sergeant Moore decided that individual would be Private First Class John Garcia. By the time Garcia had secured what was needed, the weather had taken a dramatic turn for the worse. It was recommended all flights be grounded. The two pilots that were to fly the mission let courage win out over good judgement. Because Garcia's wife had recently delivered a daughter, he now looked at risk through a different set of eyes.

When he questioned his First Sergeant about the safety of flying in what appeared to be a white-out, Harvey Moore agreed with his assessment. His decision came quickly. "I'll take your place" he told the young soldier. Twenty minutes later when the helicopter crashed into a desolate lake in the desert of Utah, another leader had given the ultimate.

There are many who would rush to declare his actions heroic. Harvey Moore would not be one of them. Yes, his death came as a result of leadership but the motive that precipitated his action is not unique.

From the fields of Gettysburg, to the trenches at Verdun, from assembly lines in the industrial heartland, to executive suites from coast to coast, leaders have sacrificed themselves for those they led, since the act of leading began.

While I have said "leadership is about creating energy" I may have overstated my case. In retrospect it may be nothing more than putting others first. And when you have, you might find, you will be remembered, in the hearts and minds of those that followed . . . forever.

APPENDIX:

SPECIFICALLY SPEAKING

If you were wondering how I feel about some other issues that relate to teambuilding, I gladly give you my thoughts on:

FIRST IMPRESSIONS: Don't hide your light under a bushel basket. Whatever strengths you have, put them on display. People want to have confidence in those they follow. Past experiences, personal philosophy, associations and reputation all help a paint a picture of you. If you don't look, think, or act like Douglas MacArthur the next best thing is to quote him.

REWARDS: Make the payoff worth the effort. People don't need a Wharton degree to do a cost-benefit analysis. History records Santa Claus developed a team while Scrooge developed a guilty conscience.

DELEGATION: When you delegate responsibility you allow others to develop skill. It also communicates trust. In addition, it frees up time for you to focus on more important issues. I've found people feel much better about me trying to improve their life than helping them do their job.

TROUBLEMAKERS: Troublemaking is not about causing problems, its genesis is malicious intent. I've found most troublemakers have been indulging their craft since their formative years. I've also discovered more often that not, I am incapable of changing their natural tendency. Because of that, I find the best way to deal with them is through exorcism. In the interim while I'm building my case, I let no misdeed go unaddressed. Trouble begets trouble.

LOYALTY: You have no obligation to be loyal above and beyond what is earned. While it has been said to be disloyal to your leader is an act of betrayal, I would suggest in some circumstances it's good judgment. When you align yourself with bad leadership decisions you jeopardize your own credibility.

MISTAKES: They come with raising MAPPs. In my life of making mistakes, the knowledge I've gained from them has always had more value than what I learned from success. I only have a problem with mistakes when they are repeated.

TENURE: There is no free lunch. I expect everyone to carry their share of the load. To allow nonperformers to remain a part of my team is to let the majority be held captive by the few.

EXTRACURRICULAR INTERESTS: The least effective people I have encountered in my life have been mono-dimensional. Finding solutions to problems requires knowledge in areas that transcend your immediate surroundings. Family, friends, hobbies, and other interests broaden horizons, develop ancillary skills and energize bodies. The only thing anyone should ever be questioned about is results.

ATTITUDE: It has always been more important to me than credentials. Given the proper mindset most people will perform. Individuals with bad attitudes tend to, not only operate at a fraction of their ability, but also contaminate those around them.

PRAISE: A four hour workout will burn up more calories than a lifetime of saying thank-you.

MICRO MANAGEMENT: When you micro manage you retard development and communicate distrust.

DECEIT: It is mankind's most vile form of behavior.

YES PEOPLE: A.K.A Whipped Dogs. Find out why and fix them.

PAPERWORK: At best, it is a depletor.

PRIDE: There may be no greater catalyst for energy.

OPPORTUNITY: Most people are capable of doing most things. Brain surgery, rocket science and having babies are exceptions.

ABOUT THE AUTHOR

Steve Sullivan is the author of *Selling at Mach 1* and *Leading at Mach 2*. His unique perspective on *Leading* and *Selling* is a product of his diverse background. Army Ranger, National Sales Manager at International Paper Company, Executive Vice President of Williamhouse-Regency, Founder of Osoli Inc, nationally recognized Motivator and award winning Author are a few highlights on his résumé. His first book *Selling at Mach 1* was a 1994 Business Book of the Year selection. He has been described as one of the most insightfully entertaining authors in America today. He holds a BA from the University of Florida and a Masters in Systems Management from the University of Southern California.